Dear Fellow Associate:

Since starting with Trane in 1970 I have seen a great deal of change. Our business has grown from manufacturing and supplying HVAC equipment to now include service, parts, building automation, and performance contracting. Today we are changing again, becoming a Comfort System Solutions Provider with a focus on the building owner as the *end* customer along with our traditional contractor/engineer customer base.

The forces of change are greater today than ever and so are the opportunities. To continue our success as a world class organization we must work to become seamless, process oriented, and more team based.

I believe our next challenge is to create an environment at Trane that will enable this transformation. It will take all of us working together to accomplish this goal. That is why we have presented you with a copy of this book. *A Journey into the Heroic Environment* is not just a title, but it speaks to the challenge at hand. Please enjoy the book and join us on the journey.

Sincerely,

Jim Schultz
Executive Vice-President,
NACG

"*A Journey* . . . is truly a winner . . . it approaches the business world with new-found trust and courage. It reads like a short story but has organic power and relevance to the ever-changing environment in which we all compete.

The concept of the Heroic Environment is the 'Open Marriage' of business philosophy . . . it borders on organization without ego.

Very simply, your eight Heroic principles say . . . do what is right, treat others as you would expect to be treated . . . with trust and dignity. It really deals with the essence of down-to-earth values."

> JIM STEVENS, Former Executive Vice President
> and Chief Operating Officer,
> Coca-Cola Enterprises

"I greatly enjoyed and appreciated your book. It cuts to the very heart of what is ailing American business today and gives some steps that can be taken to change the present course. I have since passed the book on to many others who have the same response. Thanks!"

> LOREN LANDAU, Former Coordinator of Quality,
> Texaco Refining and Marketing, Inc.

"It strikes me that the principles of the Heroic Environment and Heroic behavior are the kind of logical common sense fundamentals of life that too often get lost in big business."

> ROGER D. MISSIMER, Senior Vice President,
> R.R. Donnelley & Sons Co.

"Whether you're a CEO, a manager, a salesperson, or simply a dedicated employee, treat yourself to a personal journey into the Heroic Environment. For a change, see how well you can handle a big dose of good news, vital research, crystal-clear guidance, and exhilarating predictions. I hate to spoil the book by revealing the ending, but it turns out that the surest path to organizational success in the 1990s springs simply and naturally from our best instincts as good human beings. By the last page I felt as if I had climbed out of the trenches and taken a nice warm shower in the Truth. Those who own, operate, or manage any business, big or small, should make a point of reading this book—because you can rest assured that this is one business book your employees will be reading."

> DANIEL W. ZADRA,
> Compendium, Inc.

"Over the past 20 years, I've been teaching and training men and women how to build effective personal relationships. Your book is the freshest, most insightful work I've come across in a long time. It explains simply what a healthy relationship means at an organizational level."

> ELLEN KREIDMAN, author of the bestselling
> *Light His Fire*

"Rob Lebow has created a wonderful approach to simple age-old truths in his book, *A Journey into the Heroic Environment*. In my opinion, Rob holds the key to organizations that will do exceptionally well in the '90s. It's must reading and must implementing."

> ROBERT B. OLSON, President,
> the Benedictine Development Corporation

A Journey into the Heroic Environment

Revised and Expanded

A Personal Guide for Creating a Work Environment Built on *Shared Values*

Rob Lebow

PRIMA PUBLISHING

PRIMA PUBLISHING and colophon are registered trademarks of Prima Communications, Inc.

Library of Congress Cataloging-in-Publication Data

Lebow, Rob.

A journey into the heroic environment: a personal guide for creating a work environment built on shared values / Rob Lebow. — Rev. and expanded.

p. cm.
ISBN 0-7615-0909-7
1. Job satisfaction. 2. Work environment. 3. Quality of work life. 4. Labor productivity. I. Title.
HF5549.5.J63L43 1996
658.3'14—dc20 96-42039
CIP

97 98 99 00 01 HH 10 9 8 7 6 5 4 3 2 1
Printed in the United States of America

How to Order:

Single copies may be ordered from Prima Publishing, P.O. Box 1260BK, Rocklin, CA 95677; telephone (916) 632-4400. Quantity discounts are also available. On your letterhead, include information concerning the intended use of the books and the number of books you wish to purchase.

Visit us online at http://www.primapublishing.com

Lebow Company-owned Trademarks:
Heroic Environment®
8 Values of the Heroic Environment®
8 Principles of the Heroic Environment®
Third Generation Training®

Lebow Company-owned Copyrights:
Shared Values Process™Operating System
People Systems™
People Values™
Business Values™
Values-Based Practices™
Values-Based Decision Making™
Values-Based Consensus Building™
Group Models™
Systemic Models™
Customer Focused Self-Managing Process Groups™
Values & Attitude Study™
Value Tension Index™
VTI Score™

Contents

Contents

Acknowledgments

It's been ten interesting years since my friend Roger Parker wandered into my office one afternoon in October of 1985 and asked me what my true purpose was at work. Since that time, Roger has become a well-established authority on desktop publishing, and our fledgling discovery about the Heroic Environment® has grown into an international training and consulting business on four continents: North America, Africa, Europe, and Australia.

On a personal note, my then two-year-old daughter is now twelve (going on twenty-five) and my wife, Sharon, and I are practicing acting Heroically, something parents who read this book can understand in their own way. People have asked me to write a book on the family and to focus on *Personal Heroics*. I am encouraged by these requests and have assembled a series of guidelines on the eight Heroic Values which individuals and families can use. If you would like a complimentary copy of these family and personal guidelines, please contact us.

This book has helped shape our lives and the world we live and work in. Many kind and wonderful compliments have been showered on the book. It has been enlightening to see and hear all the ideas, reactions, and enthusiasm surrounding this project. Close to 500 individual organizational sites have studied Heroic behavior. Many have decided to embrace its simplicity of *doing what's right* for individuals, customers, the group, their organization, and their community.

A simple idea has grown in importance, and this is just the beginning. **Shared Values** has become a "buzz-phrase" around the world. In 1985, we couldn't give this idea away. Now the Shared Values Process™ Operating System (SVP™/OS) has gained respect and interest from both business and government. Uses for Shared Values are multiplying.

In 1996, the film rights were purchased by a Hollywood production group. The film, "A Journey into the Heroic Environment," recently premiered at the American Society of Training and Development (ASTD) in Orlando, Florida, to an enthusiastic audience. If you enjoy the book, you will love the movie.

There are many new friends who have been attracted to Shared Values and the ideals of Heroic behavior portrayed in the book. We are grateful for their commitment and friendship and wish them well on their journey. For those who have read the first edition of this book, you will note that we have salted this version with new ideas and several new chapters. We hope you enjoy the added chapters, and we look forward to your comments. At the end of this new version, we have created a quiz which you can take to identify the level of Heroic behavior in your organization or relationships.

During the formation of our company, we considered it important to benchmark each work environment we touched with our philosophy. Today, we are pleased to present the *Heroic Environment Quiz*, the most definitive indexing device on Shared Values in the world.

We invite you to share the results of your organization's level of Heroic behavior with us at: http://www.heroicenvironment.com, by phone at (800) 423-9327, or fax us at (206) 828-3552. We welcome a more in-depth conversation about your results to help benchmark your organization's opportunities to become a Heroic Environment. And if your results are not what you hoped for, we may be able to help you and your organization on your journey.

Each day, we have the opportunity to create our Heroic Environment anew—I with my family, colleagues, and clients, and you with your family, organization, and customers. We wish you an interesting and fulfilling journey toward your Heroic Environment, and we know that with persistence and courage you will find what you are looking for.

One final note: Sigmund Freud suggested that "True insanity is continuing to do what we have always done while expecting a different outcome." Shared Values now gives us the opportunity to do things differently—and achieve more satisfying results.

Chapter 1

The Journey Begins

Today would be a special day for John Spencer. He had just completed a job interview with a firm in Chicago, and things had gone well. The president of the company had taken the time to interview him personally, and John felt that this new company was trying hard to woo him away from his present organization. It was a good feeling and John wanted to savor the moment for as long as he could. "Not bad, Spence," he reflected quietly with some pride and self-importance.

The weather in Chicago was always unpredictable, especially in the winter. That morning, as he began his interview, the sky had been clear and the smell in the air crisp and fresh. Five hours later, John looked up at the sky in the company's parking lot, and those pleasant conditions had dramatically changed. When he entered the cab it was already snowing and he knew that O'Hare Airport would be a zoo. By the time he arrived at his terminal, the snow had turned into a blizzard and his flight and hundreds of other flights had been canceled. The terminal was packed with travelers and John felt very alone for the first time since coming to Chicago.

"Great," John thought to himself, "Now what?" After a moment's indecision, that feeling of loneliness disappeared as John grabbed a phone and called Amtrak's 800 number.

On the fifth ring an operator picked up his call. "Thanks for calling Amtrak, how may we help you?"

"Hi, do you have any sleeper compartments still available going to Denver today?"

"Yes we do, sir. May I have your name?" the operator asked. The California Zephyr would become John's home for the next sixteen hours.

"Great," John said to himself, "at least that is taken care of. I'd better call Kathy and tell her the new plan." He hung up the pay phone and immediately picked it up again. He dialed his home number in Denver.

"Hi, honey. Yeah, it went great. Listen, I'm stuck in this snowstorm at O'Hare and I'll be taking the train home. I'll arrive in Denver at 9:38 A.M. tomorrow. I've got to run. Oh, and plan on thinking about a move to Chicago, Kathy. Okay, we'll talk about it when I get home. I know it's a big move. I love you. See you tomorrow."

The cab to the Amtrak station crawled through the blinding snow.

In spite of the hassle, John felt a guilty pleasure. He loved trains and saw this as an adventure. John secretly welcomed the train ride. He had a lot of sorting out to do. This snowstorm would give him the time he needed.

From the responses he received, his interview had seemed successful. Yet, John was still unsure of what to do. Kathy, his wife, was happy at her advertising job and he loved Denver and the three-year-old home they lived in. His father had worked for the same company from the time he had left the Army until his retirement, forty-three years later. Yet John, in the eight years since he graduated from college, had already worked for two companies and was now considering moving to a third. Somehow, he didn't feel right about that. What about loyalty? He just didn't know.

He was a successful and loyal employee. John's career at his existing plant was a good one. The year before, he had been named assistant plant manager of the company's second largest electronic components parts division. But he was in a difficult industry that was changing dramatically. Most of the competitors were already overseas and John didn't know how long it would be before his firm made that same fateful decision.

They said they *never* would, but he and the other managers had their doubts. He felt the company recognized him, but he had an unexplained feeling of helplessness and frustration about what was happening around him. He could not put his finger on the problem, nor could he explain his feelings of uneasiness.

A large part of his frustration came from the fact that he had been given a great deal of responsibility to carry out the existing policies without the ability to change or modify their impact on the needs of his people. *How could people in the Connecticut home office possibly know or appreciate the market conditions in Denver? How could they make decisions and policies which affected him and the other workers without even asking for input?* And when they did ask, he felt they only did so for public relations reasons. Somehow he knew they had already made up their minds.

In the four-and-one-half years John had been at the plant, the Connecticut office had instituted program after program to fix the Denver plant. Yet nothing changed. Maybe they used different words, but the outcome was the same. The company's rigid top-down approach to decision making had made implementing new ideas almost impossible, and John knew he was being asked to enforce approaches that he felt were working against the organization's best interests.

"A train trip will give me a chance to sort all this out," John thought as he boarded the ramp. His compartment, 417-C, was two car lengths away. He had to weave slowly down the narrow passageway through the throngs of holiday travelers. Everyone seemed to be carrying full suitcases, duffels, and shopping bags. He smiled because it looked more like an evacuation of Chicago from the impending attack of some great made-in-Hollywood monster.

When he arrived at his semiprivate compartment, John's companion for the sixteen-hour journey was already comfortably seated next to the window watching the people in the crowd move to their respective destinations. John looked for a place to store his carry-on luggage. Above his companion's head was a silver rack. As John moved forward to lift his bag, the stranger turned his head and rose, with his hand instinctively stretched to support the bottom of John's bag.

While taking off his overcoat and suit jacket, John glanced at his fellow passenger. He didn't understand why, but the stranger seemed to be someone with whom he knew he would immediately feel comfortable. There was a disarming quality about the older man. John was surprised at himself—his typical response to a stranger was to be standoffish and reserved.

As the young man sat down, the older man extended his hand to introduce himself. "Hi, I'm Stan Kiplinger, but everyone calls me Kip." The gentleman's steel-blue eyes looked directly at John, as if he were trying to read him. Those eyes revealed an astuteness and a sense of playful curiosity lying just beyond their friendly twinkle.

As they shook hands, John introduced himself and added, "I don't normally take the train, but it was a mess at O'Hare and I couldn't see sleeping on one of the chairs all night. I'm tired and it's been a really long day."

"Do you travel by train often?" Kip asked.

John understood that the question was a subtle way for this stranger to begin a conversation. He did not welcome Kip's motives because he wanted to rest and contemplate his decision about the new Chicago opportunity. John's response to the older man was short. "Listen, I'm really tired. It's been a long day for me. Okay?" At that, John picked up the morning paper he had taken from the floor of the front door of his hotel room earlier that day and hid behind it. A moment later, John put the paper on his lap and turned to his companion.

Realizing that his earlier remarks were a little brusque and unfriendly, John began again. "Listen, I'm sorry if I came off short with you. I've got a lot on my mind, but I shouldn't take it out on you. I'm sorry." With that, John smiled a false smile, hoping the man would accept his apology.

Kip nodded in an understanding way. He smiled and reflected aloud that when he started in business there was little choice but to go by train. In the late 40s and early 50s he had switched to airplanes for efficiency, but they never allowed him time to reflect. Now that he had more time, he'd returned to this mode of transportation. "Yes, there is something about train travel which is missing in airplanes." Smiling, the older man continued. "Trains are a great place to sort things out, you know. Are you going home for the holidays?"

10

John nodded. "My family and I have lived in Denver for the past five years, and we really like it. Kathy, my wife, has a good job, and we have a really nice house."

"Were you in Chicago on business—I hope you don't mind my asking?"

"Not at all. I was here for a job interview." John felt himself unusually eager to talk with this stranger.

Kip nodded knowingly. "I did my fair share of looking when I was your age," he said.

"And did you ever find what you were *really* looking for?" John asked in a hopeful voice.

"No sir, I never did!" said Kip.

John felt the air go out of his throat, "Oh."

It was apparent that the small talk was over, and Kip sensed that he was being asked a serious question, one to which his young companion was seeking an answer. He paused a moment before responding. "I never did find that perfect job. Not the one you're referring to. But I found something even better."

The young man's posture changed. John was leaning forward, listening to Kip and hoping to hear something useful and important.

"It took me a long time to realize that there was no such thing as the right job. All jobs have pluses and minuses. I learned that it is possible to find fulfillment and happiness in almost any job. In fact, I *guarantee* that you can, too!"

Although John tried not to show it, he was flabbergasted by the man's answer and could not command the words necessary to respond for a long time. Here he was, after two unfulfilling job experiences, agonizing over his career, possibly leaving his home and asking his wife to sacrifice her job, one she really loved, and move halfway across the country, and this stranger was talking about job satisfaction as if it were within everyone's grasp.

John's skepticism overtook his politeness. "Just like that!" He snapped his finger in front of the man, immediately regretting the edge in his voice. "You think I can find my perfect job? I don't even know what I am looking for!"

The old man smiled almost enthusiastically. "I understand your frustration and skepticism. After all, that has always been the problem—what to look for."

At that moment, John and Kip were jolted as the train lurched forward on the journey that lay ahead. For a moment the conversation was overshadowed by the sheer force of the train's momentum. John stared out the window, the train's movement mesmerizing him. Yet, he kept thinking about Kip's outlandish guarantee. "How could he be so enthusiastic and confident?" John wondered. Everything in the young man's mind kept blurring into a series of flashes: His family's reluctance to leave Denver, his most recent interview in Chicago, his father's loyalty to *his* company, and finally John's hunger to experience a work situation that could give meaning and purpose to his life. As his mind churned with these thoughts, his uncertainty grew.

The silence was broken by Kip's words. "I hope you're enjoying the train ride. Most people find the motion and sounds soothing."

Kip's voice brought John back to the present. Without replying, John abruptly asked, "Mr. Kiplinger . . . Kip, were you serious about what you said?"

"You mean about guaranteeing that you can be happy and fulfilled in your job?" Kip chuckled. "When I was your age, I was just as frustrated and skeptical as you."

"What changed?"

"I was lucky. During my early years I came across several people who helped shape my thinking and outlook. One of those people was a man I met on a train ride. Come to think of it, not unlike this one. I was explaining to him, with a great deal of reasons, what was wrong with my job—why the employees were unhappy, why it was management's fault, and finally, why I deserved better. His name was Dan Turner. He was a sales manager from Rochester, Minnesota, and he was responsible for the east coast distribution of his company's product line.

"Anyway, as I spoke, outlining every reason in the book why I was justified to be unhappy, his face kept getting redder until finally he blurted, 'And what are you doing to improve the work environment for you and your people?' I was stopped in my tracks by this question. What did this have to do with me? I couldn't affect the work environment. I carried out the policies. I didn't have any authority or power to change anything! After all, I was just a young man at the bottom of the totem pole. I didn't have a college education, nor was I in management. The work environment wasn't my responsibility. Mr. Turner continued, rather harshly, 'Young man, stop looking for the perfect job. Instead, help your company create a better work environment.'"

John broke in, "What did he mean by that? Did he expect you to change the work environment all alone?"

"No, John," Kip's voice showed impatience, as if for a moment he had become Dan Turner. "Turner believed that the secret to job satisfaction is the way you treat others and how it causes others to treat you. Over the years, your job-related tasks change, but the environment you work in becomes more important in finding fulfillment in your work life. He went on to suggest that the essence of this idea centers around the values we share with others.

"Over the years, I have met other people who reinforced in me the sense that our Shared Values about our work hold the key to our greatest job satisfaction. I believe this is the right way of thinking about job satisfaction. It is almost entirely dependent on a work environment which is created by individuals within the organization who agree to agree on what these values mean to them personally."

John was almost disappointed in what he heard. He had always felt that job satisfaction was related to other things. He had never considered the work environment a factor in achieving job satisfaction nor had he ever considered Shared Values as a factor for his job satisfaction. He thought all business environments were pretty much the same and that values were best left at home.

"Kip, I'm not sure I agree. I don't get it. My job isn't exciting anymore. What does that have to do with the work environment? From my experience, job satisfaction is tied to things like duties, title, power, not to mention salary. Business is business. I don't really see a place for values at work. At home yes, but at work . . . well, I'm just not sure."

At that moment a sharp knock on the door broke the flow of conversation. A porter in a starched white serving jacket stuck his head in the door and asked if they were going to want an afternoon snack. Kip turned to John and said, "Their pies are great; would you care to join me?"

John nodded. At that, the older man rose to his feet in anticipation and they both started the long walk back to the dining car.

On the way to their table, John realized that his concept of job satisfaction and Kip's couldn't be further apart.

Chapter 2

Defining
the
Heroic
Environment

Once they were seated at a table in the train's dining car, John was handed a menu by the waiter. Kip turned to John and said, "Where were we?"

John put down the menu and said as respectfully as he could, "You were telling me that my job satisfaction is tied to the Shared Values in my work environment, and I wasn't buying it. I don't find my job satisfying anymore. I feel I'm not allowed to be creative or to do those things I believe are the right things to do. What does this have to do with a better work environment or the values I share with my co-workers?"

"Look, John," Kip's voice regained its earlier warmth, "in the beginning, all jobs are exciting, just like a new marriage. But typically, the thrill of newness wears off and the atmosphere becomes more political. People begin to worry more about protecting their position in the organization than about excelling."

John nodded in agreement.

Kip continued, noting that he had John's attention again. "It seems that many people have their own agendas. They blame others for their mistakes instead of taking responsibility and they only do those things that make them look good in the eyes of management.

"But contrary to what you might think, most people don't want to be small-minded. They want to make a difference. They want to believe that what they do contributes to something bigger than their own self-interest—that they can be of benefit to others. It's just that most work environments, instead of fostering unselfish behavior, discourage this very vital drive in people. I believe that people want to be great. I don't believe that anyone gets up in the morning looking forward to failure. We all want a place in the sun, and most of us want to share in the satisfactions of success with those who we care most about.

"Imagine what would happen in a work environment if people were given the freedom to act the way they really wanted to act—with courage, creativity, and independence from fear of criticism, or worse. And when people are motivated as a result of the respect and appreciation they feel, they want to contribute even more, to rise to their true potential. I call that kind of place, a place where people act heroically, a Heroic Environment. A Heroic Environment is a place that nurtures such a response in those who work there. Playing at the top of your game becomes the standard. You can't imagine how happy people would be in such a place."

"Oh yes I can," said John. "Do places like that exist? Or is that just an idea?"

"Yes, of course they do," said Kip, smiling. "True, they are all too rare, but they do exist."

"But how can one find such an environment?" persisted John. "Or better yet, how can someone like me help create such an environment?"

Kip could hardly suppress his pleasure at hearing this question from his young companion. He now knew that his instincts about John's leadership qualities were not misplaced. "That's such a good question, John, but are you sure you want to hear about how to create a Heroic Environment?"

"I've got all the time in the world, at least until I arrive in Denver tomorrow morning."

"Before we plunge into this, let's take a moment to order and refresh ourselves."

As Kip ordered his hot chocolate and John his coffee, John glanced out the window of the dining car. The unexpected blizzard had turned the fields of the Illinois countryside into a picturesque land of snow. A white carpet stretched as far as the eye could see, interrupted only by the pulsating rhythm of electric poles whisking by. John could feel a new optimism swelling in his chest, but he was not quite ready to let go of all his doubts. If only what he was hearing were possible, he reflected.

"John," Kip said, "to answer your question about creating a Heroic Environment, let me first tell you where the name originates. In ancient Greece, heroes were those who acted unselfishly, who put the interests of others before their own. I am convinced that such nobility is an integral part of most human beings. Most people rise to the occasion when treated with respect, trust, and dignity.

"But to create a Heroic Environment, all individuals in the organization must agree to follow certain fundamental principles. There are only eight of them, but they are all critical. *If even one of these principles is missing, you don't have a truly Heroic Environment.*"

Kip fell silent for a moment. He realized that he was about to share with John what had taken a lifetime to learn. He could only hope that the young man would appreciate his offering.

"John, are you sure you want to hear all this?"

"Kip, you have no idea how much!"

Reassured, Kip found an extra paper napkin and started jotting down:

The Eight Principles of the Heroic Environment®

1. Treat others with uncompromising truth.

2. Lavish trust on your associates.

3. Mentor unselfishly.

4. Be receptive to new ideas, regardless of their origin.

5. Take personal risks for the organization's sake.

6. Give credit where it's due.

7. Do not touch dishonest dollars.

8. Put the interests of others before your own.

John turned the napkin so he could read it more easily. It seemed a long while before he looked up. "You know, Kip, what you've written here is not new. But I have never worked in a place that practices this philosophy. Oh, sure, everyone uses the right words. But there's usually such a gap between words and deeds that no one takes them seriously. To actually put these principles to work, that *would* be something."

"Good, John," Kip answered. "You understand how important it would be to implement and use these principles. So let's get into some detail.

"The first principle of the Heroic Environment is *treat others with uncompromising truth*. What do you think that means?"

"I guess it means that everyone is told the truth all the time—that whether the news is good or bad, all the team members are informed about what's going on instead of being left in the dark, or worse, deceived."

Kip nodded. "Really, there *is* no other practical and sensible way to treat people. After all, if there's bad news, people find out anyway. Keeping the truth from teammates only causes anger and mistrust in the long run. On the other hand, telling the unvarnished truth early on brings the members of the team closer together and creates supporters instead of bystanders. And when everyone on the team is involved in solving the problem, the chances for success increase."

"I wish my company's top management practiced this principle," replied John, who was used to hearing bad news from the grapevine, not from the top.

Kip continued. "The second principle is *lavish trust on your associates*. Notice that I'm not just saying trust people, I'm talking about trusting them and making them *feel* trusted. Do you remember the very first time someone you respected showed you how much he or she trusted you?"

John thought for a second. His eyes brightened with the recollection. "It was my dad. He had just brought home his new Oldsmobile. I was sixteen and had recently passed my driver's education program. Dad handed me the keys and said, 'Why don't you take her for a spin, son?'"

"How did it feel?" asked Kip.

"On one hand, great. I felt so grown-up. But on the other hand, I knew I would rather die than disappoint him. No teenager has ever driven a car more carefully."

"That's *exactly* what I'm talking about," Kip said with enthusiasm as he rose from his chair. "When people *feel* trusted, they'll do *almost anything under the sun* not to disappoint the person who gave them the gift of trust."

John nodded with perfect understanding.

"Now let's talk about the third principle, a rather interesting one—*mentor unselfishly*. Let me tell you . . . "

"Well, this one I know something about," John interrupted. "I had a mentor in my first job. He was my boss. He was unhappy with my disorganized writing style—he couldn't understand my memos and reports. So he set aside several hours to help me and then kept monitoring and evaluating my writing. He kept doing this with me for several months until I became quite a good memo- and report-writer."

Kip smiled, "Good, you do understand something about mentoring. But there is much more to it. Let's take a look at the origins of the word. It is a Greek word that comes from Mentor, the loyal friend and adviser to Odysseus. You see, mentoring goes beyond teaching someone a skill. True mentoring involves teaching, advising, and befriending. Under this definition, do you currently have a mentor, and more important, are *you yourself* mentoring anyone else?"

John shook his head.

Kip continued. "In a Heroic Environment, everyone is responsible for mentoring others."

John was puzzled. "Wait a minute. What do you mean *everyone* is responsible for mentoring? I thought that only *managers* should act as mentors to their subordinates."

"In most organizations that's the way it is. But in a Heroic Environment, people mentor unselfishly because they understand that their success depends on the success of everyone on the team.

"Here's an example. Let's say you are leading a convoy of ships. It is wartime, and the ships must stick together for maximum mutual protection. Most of your ships can travel at eighteen knots per hour, but two can travel at only ten knots. How fast would your convoy travel?"

"That's easy," said John. "Ten knots."

"Right. Even though you've got ships that can go much faster, you're required to slow them down to keep in formation."

"I get it," said John. "Organizations aren't much different, are they? If you have people who are lagging behind in knowledge and understanding, the whole organization slows down. The faster you can get everyone up to speed, the faster the business progresses. Isn't that right?"

Kip smiled approvingly.

"But still, isn't training the responsibility of management?"

"Theoretically, yes, of course. But there aren't enough hours in the day for management to do it alone. Each day, there are literally hundreds of ways co-workers can help each other gain more information and understanding. In the Heroic Environment, everyone is a mentor because everyone has something to contribute. Employees also mentor their managers without fear of any negative consequences. Heroic bosses know they have much to learn from their staff."

"Okay, I think I get it," said John, looking down at the napkin. "Isn't this next value, *be receptive to new ideas, regardless of their origin,* related to the previous principle?"

"Yes. In a Heroic Environment, ideas can spring from all corners. In fact, everyone learns to listen to new ideas regardless of their origin. No one has a monopoly on good ideas. They may come from fellow workers, vendors, consultants, articles, books, and, most important, from customers. It's hard to believe, but in our fast-changing world, there are still many organizations that act as if the only good ideas come from the home office. Not only does this approach shut out good ideas, it also puts too much pressure on the managers."

"I know exactly what you're talking about," John said bitterly. "Three months ago I sent a detailed proposal to my company's home office. It took me a week of extra work at home to prepare. You know what? They didn't even bother to reply."

Kip nodded. "And how did that make you feel?"

"Rotten. In fact, that might have been the last straw that made me decide to look for another job. One thing's for sure, I won't go out of my way for them again."

"You are the perfect example of what I mean. When an organization is not receptive to new ideas, they are losing potentially vital information. Just as important, they are demoralizing their most talented, creative workers. And *when ideas are no longer proposed, the organization becomes brittle and vulnerable to market forces.* It's an organizational version of hardening of the arteries."

"The next principle really baffles me," said John. "What do you mean by *take personal risks for the organization's sake?*"

"Have you ever heard people say 'play it safe, why take a risk?' This is the attitude you find in lots of organizations, and it's the kiss of death. Risk-taking is one of the most vital activities an organization must engage in if it is to survive and thrive. An organization must encourage its members to put themselves on the line by allowing them to express their ideas without fear of ridicule, or worse. This concept is important for two reasons: First, individuals need to be challenged for their own personal growth and second, an organization unwilling to look at problems from fresh perspectives is an organization unable to respond to change."

John knew what Kip was talking about. Soon after he had started his first job, he saw the career of a bright manager ruined because he championed an idea that was out of favor with his immediate bosses. The frustrating thing was that the very same idea enabled the company's leading competitor to substantially increase its market share. He also remembered the time a new employee commented on how his former company would have solved a problem. His reward was an icy stare from his supervisor and the response, "Well, that's not how we do it around here." John still had a question. "Suppose someone has an original idea, the organization implements it, and it fails?"

Kip nodded in understanding. "*Of course* it is important that the organization makes every effort to implement ideas that work. But on a controlled basis, it's essential that people be allowed to fail when they take the risk of staking a claim. Obviously, the more talented people will make more right decisions and should be rewarded accordingly. But in a Heroic Environment, people should not be attacked for failure. After all, if the organization approves the idea, it belongs to everyone."

"Isn't the next principle the other side of the coin, *give credit where it's due?*" asked John.

"In a way you're right. Many organizations don't give people a sense that they're appreciated. On the other hand, other organizations give praise so indiscriminately that it loses its meaning. Employees want to be treated like adults, not children. More than anything, they want to feel there is a rationale for praise and promotions. They want to *understand* the rewards given and *feel* that the reward and praise system is fair."

John understood all too well. "It seems as though half the promotions given by my company are questioned by the staff. Sometimes the resentments are so strong you wonder how the plant functions at all. You'd think people would be glad to see fellow employees getting rewarded."

"In a Heroic Environment, the staff understands the reason for a promotion. While they may or may not agree with it, they don't question the innate fairness behind the reward, so they aren't resentful. In fact, in a fully functioning Heroic Environment, people are genuinely happy for their successful peers."

"Kip, I'm really curious about the next principle, *do not touch dishonest dollars.* I think I know what this means, but please explain."

"Most of us think of ourselves as honest people. Yet, I recently read a survey which concluded that over 80 percent of workers believe senior managers are to some degree dishonest. Obviously, there is a *perception* among employees that their leadership is not operating with full integrity, which means that employees can also rationalize not acting with total honesty themselves. The problems this thinking causes are horrendous, ranging from internal theft to the leaking of vital information to a competitor. And the final result of a disregard for integrity is the disintegration of the organization's morale and self-respect.

"A company with a Heroic Environment insists that all its business transactions are assessed for their ethics, not just whether the transaction is legal, but also if it is right. That's not easy in today's world. I remember a time when people would not take unfair advantage of an opponent. Today, that is not the case. Yet, of all the principles in a Heroic Environment, none is more essential."

John could feel Kip's passion welling up as he described the importance of this seventh principle. He could see some long-buried pain in Kip's eyes when he talked about the issue of integrity. But he dared not probe further. He quickly glanced down at the last principle, *put the interests of others before your own,* and said, "This sounds too good to be true."

"I won't apologize for that," said Kip, smiling. "But it is really true that when people focus their efforts on what's good for the organization as a whole rather than on their own narrow interests, everything and everyone thrives."

John sat silently for what seemed to him an eternity. Finally, he let out a low whistle. "Trying to employ all of these principles is some task, isn't it?"

"I suppose it is, John," Kip said sternly, looking at the young man with his steel-blue eyes. "But then, with all due respect to those who search for quick fixes, developing and nurturing a Heroic Environment is far too important to be trivial. What we need are people who are willing to commit themselves to the creation and sustenance of a Heroic Environment where they work. You'd be amazed at what would happen to our country's revitalization if more and more organizations were run this way."

"Kip," John's voice filled with emotion. "I can promise you that I will not forget what I'm learning here."

Kip felt a rush of paternal affection toward the young man. "Well, Pilgrim," he said with his best John Wayne imitation, "I reckon there's even more for you to learn on this here cattle run."

They both burst out laughing, mostly in relief that the emotion-laden moment had passed. Walking out of the now-empty dining car, they headed back to their compartment.

Chapter 3

Walking Our Talk—What We Allow We Teach

When they reached their compartment, John excused himself to stretch. The train ride reminded him of the long rail trip his parents once took him on to visit his mother's relatives. Gradually it all came back: the friendly people he'd met, the adventure of train travel, and the freedom he'd felt walking up and down the moving train.

He stopped to stand between two cars to feel the clatter of the train wheels and its violent gyrations. A surge of raw energy went through him as the curtain of time lifted momentarily. He now remembered that it was on that train trip that he had first kissed a girl. For a moment, he was fifteen again.

But then the magical moment passed as quickly as it had come, and his mind returned to the present. As he reviewed his extraordinary encounter with Kip, he was struck by how close he had come to settling into a mediocre career without ever finding the secret to job satisfaction.

Although he had done well by most standards, he was in a rut, and he knew it in his heart. He wanted his life to have meaning and purpose. Instead, for the past few years, he had been coasting.

Also, he felt keenly the strong competitive winds from overseas. And with his company's faltering grasp on a decreasing market share, he knew firsthand that his country's industry was in trouble. If he could only do something to bring new respect to the term "Made in America," *that* would be something worth working for!

John's mind drifted back to his job interview. Sure, he had enjoyed the warm reception he had received. But there was something too familiar about that company. He now clearly saw that their management style was not fundamentally different from the one he was thinking of leaving. Yet, somehow, it now didn't make so much difference. He was on a journey of discovery and he felt a new power. With the concepts of the Heroic Environment, maybe he could begin to feel that his career had meaning and purpose beyond that of self-interest.

John hurried back to his compartment, drawn by the power of the ideas of the mysterious Kip. He knew that he only had a few hours to master the principles that could change his life, and he didn't want to waste a moment.

As he entered the compartment, he saw Kip sitting with his eyes closed, his head resting against the window glass. Kip opened his eyes, smiled, and straightened himself up, but he remained silent.

"Kip, I have a lot of questions. Do you mind if I ask them?"

"Feel free."

"How do I go about finding a company with a genuine Heroic Environment? I think I understand what a Heroic Environment is and I believe I would know one if I saw it, but where do I look?"

Kip thought for a moment. "Many organizations have plaques on their walls proclaiming great values: 'We believe in people,' 'People first,' 'Quality is our first job,' 'We are committed to innovation,' and the like. Well, don't believe these slogans until you first talk to their people.

"In the old days, we'd call this *'walking the talk,'* and what it means is that the people who write lofty slogans should live by them. Unfortunately, that's not always the case."

"I know what you mean," said John. "When I was in school, I remember my track coach used to ride us constantly about staying in training, but the coach smoked like a chimney! After that it was hard to trust him."

"That's exactly the point," responded Kip. "Many organizations think that by putting up slogans something magical will happen. But the only thing that really changes behavior is when the proclaimed values are practiced at every level including at the top of the organization. Then, and only then, will values move down through an organization. Shared Values need to be lived, practiced, communicated, and discussed daily. John, there are two very important concepts here. First, if we live our lives in silence, there is a pretty good chance that we will send the wrong message to others. If we have established a set of Shared Values that we subscribe to, we need to establish a language that has meaning and purpose.

"Always remember: *What we allow we teach!*

"The ideas surrounding Shared Values are so important that I'm never sure where to begin. You might think of it as 'internal advertising.' After all, most businesses spend one heck of a lot of their operating budget on external advertising to attract and retain customers, but spend only pennies on their own people. John, a company's employees are the most important customers it has. The employees can never be placed in the wrong to make the external customer right.

"Let's get back to the other important point of communicating our Shared Values. And that is the issue of consistently 'walking our talk.' Setting standards around our Shared Values is the key.

Not only talking about telling the truth, but establishing guidelines around each one of our values."

"So if I understand you correctly, the way you ensure that your Shared Values are consistently practiced is to establish the standards for each of your values. Boy, that seems like a tough job," said John with some reservation.

"John, I'm afraid that there are no shortcuts in establishing Shared Values within an organization or between two people. If you are willing to accept the benefits you need to first invest the time necessary. Most organizations who practice Shared Values have invested years in the process. Now this is an important point."

As Kip spoke these words he grabbed a piece of paper to underscore his remarks. "Think of it this way. Most organizations go for the quick fix! They don't mean to, and they believe they are doing what's right. They introduce a program to fix this or that in hopes it will stick."

John interrupted him. " 'Program of the year' is what we call them," he said with a mocking smile.

"And how do they work?" asked Kip, already knowing the answer to his question.

"They aren't doing what we hoped they would do. But they keep on coming," said John, as they both smiled. "First we had *Management by Objectives,* then they threw *Quality Circles* at us, followed by *Total Quality Management.* We are just finishing up *ISO/QS 9000* and they are priming us for *Open Book Management* and *Activity-Based Management.* We've been Benchmarking other organizations for the past few years observing how other operations are employing *Process Engineering* and we will be starting to introduce something Connecticut calls the organization's *Core Competencies.*"

John's mood turned serious. "You know even though each one of these programs seemed important to us at the time, the enthusiasm for it always trails off. It's as if something is still missing in all our efforts to change the way we do business."

Kip nodded knowingly. "Yes, there is something missing, John. Remember, I used the word *Process.* Well, I used that word for a very special reason. Organizations with the best intentions introduce programs to help support their people and their systems, unknowingly undermining, in many cases, the simple truth of every organization, regardless of size.

"In a rush to improve productivity and profits or to stay competitive in the marketplace, they ignore their greatest asset, the inherent wisdom and goodness of their people. Instead of putting in place a set of Shared Values, they focus on Programs to solve their problems and challenges. Almost all the Programs you mentioned are both worthwhile and appropriate, but they will never *stick* until everyone feels respected, safe, listened to, and valued.

"When I was growing up, my dad used to talk to me about the difference between our **Sunday Values** and our **Everyday Values.** He said, 'Kip, your Sunday Values are important only if you intend to wear them for the other six days. If not, keep your mouth shut. At least that way they won't call you a hypocrite . . . or worse!'"

"That's pretty straight talk," said John.

"Yes, and it still applies today."

"I have also heard this called *espoused values* versus *actual values*," replied John thoughtfully, "but frankly, it never made much of an impression on me before now."

Kip nodded. "Over the years, I've seen a lot of angry, disillusioned, betrayed people who never recovered their trust once they saw what was behind their management's Sunday values. Preaching without integrity is explosive stuff and needs to be handled carefully. Believe me, if you say one thing and do another, you'll eventually be found out. Great care needs to be taken in both the style and content of our actions and communications. We need to pay conscious attention to what we say and how we say it. *Words without actions and actions without words can't successfully create or sustain a Heroic Environment.*

"So to answer your question directly, the best way to check out a new company is to look at how they *walk their talk*. If a company's Sunday values and everyday values are not aligned, or in balance, go elsewhere."

"Okay, I understand," said John, "but how do I, in my position with very little power, put the concept of 'walking the talk' to use?"

"Good, you obviously understand that change does not start with them but with you! Nevertheless, your first job is to start sharing these ideas with your top management as well as your fellow employees. You see, there are two types of values that every organization has to deal with to succeed.

They are your *Business Values* and your *People Values*. These two groups define an organization's values and lie at the foundation of unlocking and discovering your Heroic Environment.

"I have come to recognize that Business and People Values are in a dynamic tension with each other. Think of them not as a core set of values, like most business schools teach, but as a scale that needs to be in balance. Values are never seen by the customer and the employees as anything other than how the organization and its representatives behave every day, especially when the organization or its people don't think anyone is watching.

"John, the greatest mistake I ever made in helping to manage my company in the early years was that I thought there was only one set of core values and that no one standing on the outside of our operation would see our inconsistencies. I came to learn the truth the hard way about core values— *they didn't exist.* What existed was the organization's everyday values. Yes, our behavior was seen and felt by everyone, whether they were our employees or our customers.

"John, I always felt that people were important, and the treatment of people was listed in our organization's set of values. But the funny thing was that every time a business decision was in conflict with how we wanted to treat our people, we decided in favor of the business, and was that a big mistake! We seemed to always pay for that neglect in increased turnover, dissident behavior, lack of productivity, and decreased employee loyalty.

"It wasn't until years later that I realized that the reason we turned our back on the people wasn't because we didn't believe in what we were saying, but because we didn't understand how to balance both our Business and People Values.

"Once we started using the Eight Heroic Principles and the standards surrounding each principle, we were able to successfully manage both sets of values and reach every goal we wanted to achieve."

At that, Kip took some paper from his briefcase and started to draw the first of several charts. By this time, John was recognizing the importance of

Kip's words and had decided not to interrupt him with any questions when Kip said, "here are some rough examples of a set of Business Values."

	Business Values	
	Directed Toward Your Outside World (External to the Organization)	
Business Values	**Individual or Group Performance**	**Organizational Performance**
• High product quality		
• Superior customer service		
• Strong community involvement		
• High ethical business practices		

"This first table lists your **Business Values.** Business Values are those things which an organization must do every day to be successful. A company's beliefs and actions concerning quality, customer service, community involvement, and business practices are good examples of what I mean. For the most part, these values are directed toward the external world. Of course, if you talk to twenty different companies you'll get twenty different sets of Business Values. But typically there are similarities.

"A simple exercise is to list your Business Values. Grade yourself and your organization on how well your performance matches your values on a daily basis. You can use a scale of one to five and see how you and your company stack up. In fact, I just put down the most universal *external values* that most organizations address.

"Now let's move on to the second set of values, **People Values.**" Kip took another piece of blank paper and started to draw the next chart.

"People Values indicate how the company believes people inside the organization should be treated."

People Values		
Directed Toward Your Inside World		
(Internal to the Organization)		
People Values	**Group Performance**	**Organizational Performance**
• Telling people the truth		
• Trusting people		
• Mentoring people		
• Being receptive to ideas		
• Taking personal risks		
• Giving credit where it's due		
• Honesty		
• Putting others first		

"These values are even more important than the Business Values, because it is your people who support and carry out the other set of your values, your People Values. If the people inside your organization don't feel that they are part of a supportive environment, a Heroic Environment, they will not take care of your Business Values, *the values that your customers see and experience.*"

As Kip drew this second rough chart, John could see that the older man was no stranger to people and to organizational evaluations. John noticed immediately that the Eight Heroic Principles were the foundation of Kip's People Values.

"John, in filling this out, use the same process as in the Business Values Chart. Between the two of these, you'd be amazed at how clearly you can diagnose your organization's strengths and weaknesses when it comes to Shared Values. And this is the key to all performance, both on a personal and organizational level.

"I've seen evidence over the years that the practice of Shared Values is linked directly to profits.

No single element will forecast the success of an operation quicker than measuring its level of Shared Values. The greatest predictor of future success is the way the operation succeeds at Shared Values.

"Remember, if there is a wide gap between your *Sunday values* and your *everyday values,* you aren't walking the talk, and the consequences of the misalignment and employee cynicism will eat you alive.

"Let me give you an example of how this applies," said Kip. "As you know, most customers don't ever meet all the people who support a retail clerk. So, in a way, you could say that the clerk is just the tip of the whole organization's iceberg. And this pretty much applies to just about every department and organization, from grocery stores to schools to hospitals, printing companies, customer service departments, and I could go on and on.

"The people we meet are pretty much the representatives of the whole organization. They are, in a way, a walking advertisement for their organization. In fact, we base our judgments about a company on meeting just a few of its people. I guess you might think of the people on the front lines as the organization's ambassadors."

"I never thought of it that way," agreed John. "But that's so true; I'd say I judge an organization by how I'm treated. And if I'm not treated well, I won't go back to the store."

"Yes, we are all like that. And yet most organizations obviously don't understand that. Why else would they take for granted these very special people? Why wouldn't organizations invest the same time and care in the overall education of these employees as they do in top management—teaching them what the organization stands for? To the outside world, these people *are* the organization! Frankly, the most important person I meet from any operation is the person who serves me." Kip waited for John to think about his last point.

"I've got an interesting story to share with you, John.

"Recently, the UPI news service reported a human interest story that was most instructive.

Somewhere on the West Coast, a plainly dressed older man caused quite a stir.

"This man was in the process of paying his parking fee when the attendant informed him that he could get his parking stub 'validated' at the bank where he'd just done some business at the ATM machine. By getting his ticket validated he could save two dollars.

"Feeling that two dollars saved was two dollars earned, the man returned to the bank to get his parking stub stamped. After patiently standing in the bank's customer line for several minutes, he self-consciously approached the next available teller and requested that his parking stub be validated. The bank clerk inquired what transaction had been processed as she suspiciously eyed the poorly dressed man. For some reason, the bank teller was not in a generous frame of mind and refused to validate his ticket. Well, the fellow was upset and started to raise his voice. A supervisor was attracted to the activity and listened to his teller's comments. Earlier that week, the supervisor had been to a company training seminar on 'team building,' and thought he knew just what to do."

ORGANIZATION-WIDE VALUES

PEOPLE VALUES

BUSINESS VALUES

"I guess he stepped in and validated the man's parking stub," said John.

"Well, that's what he wished he had done in hindsight. But instead, he followed what he had learned in his team-building class, supported his bank clerk's decision, and refused to validate the man's parking stub. Here was their reasoning: The transaction that the man had performed was a bank withdrawal on the outside of the bank at the ATM machine and was not considered a 'bank transaction.'

"Well, the man was furious and asked if a withdrawal made here and now was a bank transaction. The supervisor said that it was. So the man withdrew his life savings from the bank, got his parking stub validated, *and walked across the street and deposited a little over two million dollars in a competing bank!*" John's mouth opened wide with amazement.

Kip continued. "Here is the lesson to be learned. When we don't have our People and Business Values universally understood and in balance, we are often influenced by training programs and company policies that may be well-meaning but don't serve our customers and employees. When you add the extra ingredient of *judging people by their appearance and treating them as outsiders,* you have created a volatile recipe for failure.

"The bank had not understood the value of working with customers and had lost a valued account. Had the man been someone the teller knew, perhaps the outcome would have been different.

"How many other customers do we chase away who go silently into the night without a fuss? Yes, we all take cues from others. You know what role models are? Well, the treatment of people is a learned behavior, and one that is perpetuated through role models within all organizations. If the people we work for and with treat us with respect, then we in turn continue this behavior toward others. That is why organizations have personalities of their own. In a Heroic Environment, every employee is taught to respect others . . . "

"No, Kip," interrupted John. "They don't have to be taught to respect others, because in a Heroic Environment they learn that from the way they are treated."

Kip smiled the smile of a teacher who knew that his message was getting through.

"There are a lot of well-meaning companies that are putting together customer-service and quality-assurance programs. John, it seems to me that it would be a lot cheaper and more effective if companies *really* understood how simple the problems actually are. Introducing these programs, whether for customer service, quality control, or employee efficiency, *will not produce lasting re-sults unless you first have the proper environment in place and understand that Business Values and People Values are two separate sets of values. People Values are not a subset of an organization's Business Values, but a legitimate partner in a 'dy-namic equilibrium.'"*

Kip, realizing that he needed to clarify his point, took his pen and drew a scale. On one side of the scale he wrote "Business Values," and on the other side of the scale he wrote "People Values."

Turning to John, he said, "When both these sets or groups of values are in balance, you have a Heroic Environment. But when either your Business or People Values are top-heavy, one emphasized to the neglect of the other, your work environment will go out of balance and the dynamic equilibrium that you need will be destroyed."

John seemed to grasp the significance of Kip's drawing and explanation, but had one more question. "Kip, why do you call this balance of the two sets of values a 'dynamic equilibrium'?"

"Because it is never stabilized or fixed. Over the course of time, new priorities and situations arise that destabilize our values and challenge our beliefs, policies, and strategies. Let's say, for example, that something happens at your plant in Denver that affects the way you do business. A competitor from overseas introduces a product in direct competition to your bread-and-butter money-maker, and they cut the price by 30 percent.

"What your organization does in response, both internally and externally, will communicate more about your organization's *actual values* than any words, slogans, or plaques could."

"That would be tough to manage if it happened to us," said John.

Kip smiled and said, "John, it's not a matter of 'if,' it's a matter of 'when.' What you do about it when it happens will define whether you have a sustainable Heroic Environment or not.

"Heroic Environments are easy to create in good times. The real challenge to our principles and values comes when times get tough. The true character of individuals and organizations is best tested during challenging times."

John began to understand the greater significance of the Heroic Environment and the importance of creating a balance between the two sets of values—Business Values and People Values.

This was no pie-in-the-sky dream for creating fulfilling working conditions. *But rather, the Heroic Environment was a foundational idea, a road map for the overall success of any organization.*

Kip looked at his pocket watch after seeing that it had long since turned dark outside their window. "Well," he said, "why don't we get something to eat before we talk ourselves out of dinner?"

Chapter 4

Understanding Heroic Behavior

John would not remember his dinner that evening. He felt eager to start implementing the concepts of the Heroic Environment, but he had one overriding problem he could not solve. Kip, on the other hand, seemed to be enjoying every morsel of his pot roast. He joked with the waiter as if they were old friends, and he kept the conversation light, deflecting John's attempts to return to their ongoing discussion.

Finally, Kip put his fork down, emptied his glass of water, and folded his napkin on the table. "John, you look perplexed. What is it?"

71

"Kip, I'm overwhelmed. I would like to institute the principles of the Heroic Environment where I work, but how do I get started? I mean, they're great building blocks if the whole organization implements them. But how does someone like me, who is not the company's president or even the plant manager, start instituting change within an organization that hasn't agreed to act heroically? I feel as though I've been given a blueprint without a set of instructions."

Kip nodded. "You're right, of course. The Heroic Environment cannot be instituted until management and staff are committed to it. But in the meantime, there is a way to begin on a more modest, individual level. You can start with the group of employees you are directly responsible for, whether they number one or fifty. You first have to build a basic level of agreement among this small group, and it has to do with the way you treat them and the way they respond in kind.

"There are five individual behavior traits involved. Together, I call these five traits *Heroic Behavior*." Kip turned his place mat over and quickly penned the five traits.

Heroic Behavior

1. Give and receive permission to act with autonomy.

2. Treat others as significant.

3. Make everyone feel like an insider.

4. Trust.

5. Act with integrity.

John studied the paper. "So starting with Heroic Behavior can eventually lead to the creation of the Heroic Environment."

"Yes. It's a modest way of beginning now, of blooming where you're planted. What eventually happens is that when you put Heroic Behavior into action in your office or department, you start a process that eventually gets noticed. And that's how it all begins.

"But let's talk about the first trait, **give and receive permission to act with autonomy**," said Kip. "It's amazing how many managers tend to overmanage their employees. They don't seem to realize that by constantly hovering over their staff they are suffocating their employees' creativity and sense of adulthood. This becomes a self-fulfilling prophecy. When people are not given the chance to act responsibly, out of their own choice, they don't—they act like children. Furthermore, overbearing managers kill the sense of creativity that lies in most individuals."

"Okay, okay," John jumped in, feeling acutely uncomfortable. "To some extent you are describing me. I know that I tend to overmanage. But if I don't watch what my people are doing, how can I be responsible for the results?"

"I understand," Kip smiled sympathetically. "A good manager, like a good coach, has three tasks that must be done well. First, the manager must make sure that the team is good. Second, the manager should give the team a clear idea of the desired results. And last, the manager should give team members as much freedom as possible to succeed. Only in the case of failure should the manager ever consider reducing a team member's autonomy. Even then, as soon as the employee performs well again, autonomy should be restored; otherwise, the employee doesn't belong on the team."

"Wow," John whispered, "it's so simple, isn't it? Why do we tend to make things so complicated?"

"John, overmanaged employees are like ships with ten year's growth of barnacles on the bottom of their hulls—they create unnecessary resistance and inefficiency. In the Heroic Environment, self-management is encouraged, and responsibility is delegated downward," said Kip. "The results are a lot better, and the company grows faster. I once heard someone say, 'You can lead a thousand people, but you can't carry even three on your back.'"

"It would be amusing if it didn't hit home so hard," said John, shaking his head.

Kip continued. "The second trait is **treat others as significant.** People need to feel special and valued. What this means is that everyone in the work group is empowered with a sense of importance. Furthermore, they are also taught how to show

What Do Employees Want?

Items Rated by Employees and Employers	Rating by Employees (in order of importance)	Rating by Management (in order of importance)
1. Appreciation	1	8
2. Feeling "in" on things	2	10
3. Help on personal problems	3	9
4. Job security	4	2
5. Good wages	5	1
6. Interesting work	6	5
7. Promotions	7	3
8. Management loyalty to workers	8	6
9. Good working conditions	9	4
10. Tactful disciplining	10	7

Source: U.S. Chamber of Commerce © 1986, *The Balanced Program.*

appreciation to fellow workers. To instill this behavior is quite easy. It simply has to start with you. You'll be amazed how quickly everyone catches on.

"This brings me to an interesting survey you may have heard about. Not long ago, the U.S. Chamber of Commerce conducted a study on what employees want. They proceeded to show both employees and managers ten priorities and asked them to rate them from 1 to 10, with 1 being the most important. Let me show you the results." Kip reached into his coat pocket and removed a folded piece of paper (see page 76).

"Notice how far apart employees and managers are from each other."

John let out a low whistle. "Why is that?"

"Perhaps it's because our managers are taught principles that no longer apply today. The reason employees don't put good wages as their number one priority is that they take a decent wage for granted—we are no longer working in sweatshops. The new breed of employees is looking for more than good wages; they're seeking to be a part of an extended family of productive people, where everyone matters.

"Even today, you still hear some managers say, 'If so and so doesn't like it here, let him go elsewhere.' What foolish arrogance! Good employees are a company's most important asset. In a Heroic Environment there is no us/them mentality. Hierarchies are deemphasized. Everyone uses the term 'we' when talking about the company.

"This leads me to the third trait of Heroic Behavior: **Make everyone feel like an insider.** People need to feel that they belong, that they have 'insider' status in their workplace. Otherwise, they feel alienated."

"I'm not sure I have a handle on how this works," said John.

Kip thought for a moment. "Okay, here's a good example of how *not* to treat people. In the 70s and early 80s, as Detroit was seeing its market share eroding quickly to foreign car manufacturers, panic set in, with everyone blaming others for the problem. One plant manager decided that the problem was one of image. So he issued a memo forbidding those employees not driving a company-manufactured car from parking in the salaried employees' and guests' parking lot. 'This condition does not convey a positive image to other salaried employees or guests who visit our plant,' the memo stated, 'and it has a negative impact on our share of the car market. Henceforth, salaried workers driving the offending cars will be banished to the hourly workers' lot.'

"Now, as you know, the hourly workers are generally the assembly workers—people with more direct contact with making cars than the secretaries, managers, accountants, and other salaried staff. And they were offended. Here's what the vice president of the local union said: 'They're punishing the salaried employees by telling them to park with my people, as if *we* were dogs. A lot of us consider this offensive'."

"I bet the union had a field day with this one!" John exclaimed gleefully.

"Frankly, that's not the point. The point is that here the plant's most important asset, the people who build its cars, were treated like outsiders by an unthinking manager. It's not as if they weren't concerned about the company's problems—over a third of their friends had already lost their jobs.

"John, nobody likes to feel like a second-class citizen. I believe that people want to be part of building something important. And they want to be 'in' on decisions. That's why smart managers bring their people together to discuss problems. Often, it is the hands-on people who have the solution. *Involve employees in finding solutions and you have unleashed an invaluable resource.*"

"I think there's another way employees are left outside," added John. "In my company, I see new employees given very little instruction, and then their managers wait for them to make a mistake, which is then corrected. It's almost like the fraternity ritual of hazing: Make the task as hard as possible and see who survives."

"Yes, it's a form of withholding information, and most non-Heroic companies practice it. It's often not a conscious act, just a relic of a more oppressive past. Mentoring people from the very beginning is so important. Teach them the ropes properly, and you'll find yourself doing a lot of praising instead of criticizing.

"John, there's a saying that information is power. Many try to withhold it, believing that by doing so they become more powerful. Ironically, the reverse is true. The most powerful people throughout the ages were the men and women who *freely* gave of their knowledge. In fact, in our information age, the more information you can share with more people, the more powerful you and your group become."

John sat silently. Some of what he was hearing was painful because it revealed his failings. He had always considered himself a good manager; now he wasn't so sure. Finally, he said, "I never realized before to what extent what I *am* affects everyone who works for me. What a responsibility!"

Kip smiled, "Well, I have something that will cheer you up."

He motioned to the waiter and ordered them both a strawberry shortcake. "It's not exactly on

my diet, but our minds have been working over-
time, so let's splurge a little." Listening to Kip's
cheerful talk helped John relax. He realized how
important it was for him to earn Kip's respect.
And Kip's nonjudgmental attitude toward him
was a lesson in mentoring all by itself. As their
dessert was served, both John and Kip took the
opportunity to enjoy the punctuated silence of
the rumbling train. There was something soothing about the distant cacophony of steel rolling
over iron.

Finally, Kip settled back in his seat and began
discussing the fourth trait of Heroic Behavior.
"**Trust** acts as an empowering message to others.
In an atmosphere thick with suspicion, everyone
is afraid to react spontaneously. As a result, the
organization becomes inflexible and brittle. It
cannot adjust quickly to change.

"Trust, on the other hand, is the damndest
thing. It is hard to define, and so many people talk
about it, yet few know how to extend it. I think
that's because trust is the most Heroic of all
traits. You really have to overcome the fear of having your trust betrayed to risk trusting others. It's

a little like jumping into the darkness with the confidence that someone will be there to catch you—and that's Heroic. Is it worth it? Absolutely, because a team that trusts its members will always out-achieve a team that is ruled by distrust and intimidation. Unfortunately, most organizations try to get results from people by manipulating them instead of trusting them."

"Why is that?" asked John.

"It goes back to a different belief system about managing people. In the early 60s the buzz phrase was 'Management by Objectives.' This was a concept about how to delegate tasks and achieve results, and people got all excited about it. By people, I really mean senior managers, many of whom had been military officers and who were comfortable with wielding power and having control. So of course they got excited about a system that gave them a measurable way to control the people below them. Kind of a foolproof accountability system. The only problem was, this widely accepted technique didn't take into consideration how people really *want* to be treated and how they perform best.

"The next thing we knew, everyone was delegating and managing by objectives, but no one was extending or lavishing trust. Instead, they were controlling and acting like cops. And to make matters worse, the system included penalties for failure, all without any input from the poor devils who had to live under this 'great, new, modern system.' At that point, we had entered the era of hermetically sealed management," said Kip, smiling sadly. "In a tragic way, people were losing faith in each other.

"The major problem with all this is that we were imposing on people systems they had no control over. Crunching numbers and hitting abstract goals became all-important. Some 'experts' actually believed that since robots would eventually take over factory tasks, there was no reason to be concerned about people issues. You can pretty much trace America's competitive decline to the mentality of that time."

"I understand," responded John. "But surely, we do need standards. How do we achieve them without controlling people?"

"By developing responsibility throughout the entire organization. That way, people at all levels take on the role of quality control. And all the evidence shows that with few exceptions, people who have been extended trust will naturally respond to new and higher standards of quality, ethical behavior, fairness, personal autonomy, and creativity," said Kip.

John felt elated. "I've got it. It's so simple."

"Perhaps, but it isn't *easy*. It's not just that managers who have decided not to be 'cops' have to reorient their thinking. Employees who were treated like objects have to release their own defense mechanisms. It doesn't happen overnight."

"How do you know when you're succeeding?"

"One way is when you start hearing over and over from job applicants that they have heard about the great working conditions—and that they heard about it from your employees! That's when you know your team members are acting as the company's ambassadors.

"Now, the fifth trait of Heroic Behavior is just as important: **Act with integrity,**" said Kip.

"I hear that word so often I no longer know what it means. What's *your* definition?" asked John.

"Integrity deals with the most far-reaching question of all. It constantly asks the critical question: What does our office, our group, or our organization stand for?"

John looked perplexed.

"Let me tell you a story that will explain this," said Kip. "Not long ago, the CEO of a company and a group of his senior managers were all together in a product-planning meeting. The topic was the shipping date of a new product the company had been working on for two years. There was a pile of purchase orders waiting to be filled, and articles about the product had been written in industry magazines. Industrywide anticipation was high. Furthermore, with all the advance orders, if the product could be shipped by the end of the quarter, the company would reach the sales and profit figures it had promised Wall Street, and the CEO would be the darling of his board of directors.

"But there was a problem. The head of product development said there were glitches with the product and it would not be ready for shipment by the end of the quarter. The CEO hit the roof. Something had to be done! In his best Management-by-Objectives style he asked what other product could be shipped instead. The head of product development said there was an earlier version of the product that had several unsolved bugs but which could be resurrected. That was the only alternative."

"So what happened?" asked John.

"The CEO ordered the old prototype be shipped instead."

"But why?"

"So that they could meet their financial numbers for the blasted quarter. Now the story really heats up. When production heard that the defective product was going to be shipped, they couldn't believe their ears. Quality control put up a big stink, customer support started to gear up for an avalanche of problems, and the sales department found themselves caught up between loyalty to their company and loyalty to their customers. Now let's see what happened as a result.

"Because production felt the product was inferior, they spent all their efforts disavowing any responsibility. Quality control followed suit because they felt their concerns were overridden and because they were embarrassed by the whole affair.

"Customer support was outraged. They felt victimized in a war between unhappy customers and their company. And sales, after initial elation that their back orders would be filled, realized that what they were selling would damage their relationship with their clients for a long time."

"I can't believe all these problems weren't seen before this decision was made," John said.

"Oh, there's more," said Kip. "Public relations was the last to find out about this. They were in a bind. Should they deny the allegations about a shoddy product, or should they admit the problem? If they admitted the faults, they would have to answer to the public and press why the product was released in the first place. Or, if they denied the problem, they would risk personal and professional loss of reputation in the future. Not only that, if they coordinated their answers with other corporate departments, they could even be accused of willful wrongdoing and illegal conspiracy.

"Well, John, as you can see, one decision at the highest level to achieve some numerical goals was costing this organization its integrity, its soul. Instead of heroically telling the truth by announcing to everyone that the product would be shipping late, the company squandered the trust of its employees, vendors, and the public.

"People need to be part of something they can feel proud of," Kip said with special emphasis.

"No wonder so many employees perceive senior management as being dishonest and incompetent," exclaimed the young man.

"John, remember this well. When it comes to integrity, there are no shortcuts. As you move up the ranks, as I'm sure you will, there will be times when the pressure will be on you to perform, to achieve a goal, and you'll be tempted to take a shortcut. When that time comes, remember this moment, and do the right thing.

"But let me apply this behavior to your situation today. Suppose you are enacting Heroic Behavior with your group, and your company asks you to do something that you consider unethical; would you do it?"

John thought for a long while. "First, I would have to be certain in my mind that the order is really unethical, as opposed to one I disagree with. After all, as a member of the corporate team, I must execute many decisions I may not agree with. However, if, after much soul-searching, I could be certain it was a matter of ethics, I would use every available channel to voice my objections to my superiors."

"And risk your chances for advancement, even your job?" Kip interjected.

"Yes."

"Suppose they ignore your opposition?" pressed Kip.

"Then I would have no choice but to resign."

"You mean you would risk losing everything you've worked for for the sake of your integrity?"

"Everything I've worked for would be worth *nothing* without my integrity," John replied with special emphasis.

There was silence for what seemed like a long time.

The waiter stopped by the table with a coffeepot and the check. Kip asked when the train would arrive at the Kansas City station. The waiter looked at his watch and said they were due to arrive in two hours, around 11:00 P.M. Kip explained that the next shift would take over then and that a friend of his would be the new engineer. "Her name is Peggy Bentley. Her father and I go back a long way. In fact, I'm Peggy's godfather. When we get to the station I'd like you to meet her."

Chapter 5

The Four Corporate Personality Traits

As the two men returned to their compartment, John reached for his briefcase and wrote some notes about their dinner conversation. He wanted to make sure he wouldn't forget what he was learning. The five steps toward Heroic Behavior struck both an emotional and a rational chord, and it made sense that developing this kind of behavior would be a good first step toward creating a Heroic Environment. Yet even as he was writing, new questions were begging to be answered.

"Kip, I'm afraid you aren't quite rid of me . . . do you mind?"

"Not at all," said Kip, putting down his newspaper. "I'm just surprised you don't want to take a break from all this."

"I can't," the young man blurted out. Then, as he realized how intense he'd sounded, he smiled self-consciously. Kip returned his smile, and John relaxed.

"Okay, I now understand Heroic Behavior. Heroic Behavior creates an atmosphere where people can act Heroically, doesn't it?"

Kip nodded.

"Then would you please define for me your ideal definition of a Hero?"

"Let me start by telling you about someone I admired very much. I once worked with Max, a very special man. He developed an uncanny ability to cut right to the heart of a problem by understanding the human factors behind it. And when he would resolve a problem, he would do it with everyone's ego intact. He seemed to know exactly how to treat others.

"Max had a gift for understanding human needs. He reinforced his coworkers' sense of self-esteem without coming off as insincere. He made everyone feel important. Even if he disagreed with someone, that person would walk away from him feeling more focused and inspired. He knew how to keep the discussion on the issues, never attacking a person's sense of dignity in the process.

"At the time I was working with him, I was young and worked long hours. I thought pretty highly of myself. And yet I wasn't getting half the bottom-line results Max was. One day, utterly frustrated, I cornered him and asked directly about his success. His answer was simple, 'Kip, I put the needs of others before my own.'

"Frankly, I didn't buy it—his answer seemed far too simplistic. I dismissed his words, but I couldn't dismiss his ongoing success. I saw how his influence grew without his seeming to work at it. So I started to take more notice, and you know what? Max was right. It *was* his genuine interest in others and how others responded to him that made the difference.

"He had other virtues. He would stand up for the things and the people he believed in without fear or favor. When necessary, he would take charge, yet he much preferred to let his employees try their hand at leadership. At such times he would roll up his sleeves and become just one of the team members. As a result, those around him became experienced and confident leaders themselves. And, of course, by developing a team of capable, enthusiastic people, Max was now using minimal time supervising and maximum time creating and producing. Where I was spending 60 percent of my time making sure my team got the job done, he was spending only 10 percent—and getting better results.

"John, you should have seen his genuine happiness when he saw his co-workers succeeding. He was so optimistic. Yet he wasn't the least bit naive. He could smell a phony a mile away."

"So *that's* your model for the Hero," exclaimed John.

"Guilty as charged," Kip answered good-naturedly. "But let's generalize our discussion so that it can apply anywhere.

"Heroes make things happen. They are the men and women who tend to focus on finding solutions while others are still defining the problem. They are results-oriented, not process-oriented. And because of their 'can do' attitude, they move the whole organization forward. A Hero's motto is, 'It doesn't matter who gets the credit as long as the job gets done.' And because they are *results*-driven, not *ego*-driven, they tend to throw the limelight on others. Yet, paradoxically, Heroes become immensely powerful in a positive way. Why? Because their motives are universally trusted.

"Heroes are also facilitators of new ideas. When they discover a beneficial idea, they champion it, regardless of its source. And then they fight for its success by working toward reaching a consensus.

"The most important value of Heroes is that they create a model of behavior for others to emulate. They bring out the best in people and, as such, define the direction of the team."

As Kip was talking, he noticed a crestfallen look on John's face. He seemed distracted and fidgety. "What's wrong, John?" he asked, concerned.

John looked at Kip, shaking his head, "The more you describe the Hero, the less confident I am that I could be like that. Look," he said with an edge in his voice, "I try to put the interests of others before my own, but I don't always succeed. Nor do I often stand up for unpopular ideas in meetings, even if I agree with them . . . I haven't always acted courageously."

Kip understood. "John, acting Heroically is a process. None of us succeeds all the time, but it's a model for which we strive. And when we stray from it we can return to it."

"Okay, I can accept that," John answered. "But there's another question that's been bothering me. Can you honestly expect every member of the Heroic Environment to become a Hero in the way you just defined? What about the differences in personalities, capabilities, capacity, and even *commitment?* Do you really believe that all people see themselves as Heroes?"

Kip nodded, smiling, "You force me to get into more depth than I thought I'd need to," fully enjoying his young friend's display of honesty and keen mind. "You are absolutely right. There are different personality traits as well as different levels of capacity, commitment, and courage. The old saying that 'it takes all types to make the world go round' still applies. Let me first explain what I mean by personality traits.

"Most experts agree that our personality is a result of our genetic makeup and our past experiences, especially childhood experiences. Our personality emerges as we try to make our way in this world. Some of us learn that it is more pleasant to be liked and accepted, even if it means being like everyone else. Others feel compelled to become leaders and be admired. Yet others learn that their different way of seeing the world makes them unpopular. I believe that today kids call this type of person a 'nerd.'

"So you see, John," Kip continued, "it's important to not *judge* people for being who they are. By the time they come into contact with you in the workplace, they have developed a set of behavior patterns that helps form their basic personality. I call this the person's **Dominant Trait.**

A Balanced Work Environment

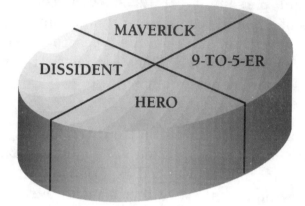

"Over the years I've found it extremely useful to think in terms of four **Dominant Traits** interacting in an organization: the **Hero**, the **Maverick**, the **9-to-5-er**, and the **Dissident.**

"I've already described my idea of the Hero, so let me tell you about the **Maverick.** Mavericks are noted for coming up with new ideas, methods, and strategies. Their ideas keep an organization or group competitive and challenged. They are the original thinkers—the poets. They represent our creative best—what we can become if we allow ourselves to dream and imagine.

"Mavericks deal with the world in two ways. Either they welcome controversy, as they flaunt their disregard for what others think—I'm sure you can think of some performers and artists as well as entrepreneurs who might fall into this category—or, as happens *much* more often, they are the poets, the dreamers, the philosophers, the scientists, and the thinkers—people who often withdraw into their own world. These creative types have learned to live without group acceptance. They are in the habit of developing new ideas on their own. Because society has always treated them as 'different,' they are generally mistrustful and have poor communications skills.

"Mavericks are some of my favorite people. Most of us believe that old saying, 'If it ain't broke, don't fix it,' until our competition leaves us in the dust. Mavericks keep us on our toes by insisting that just because 'it ain't broke' doesn't mean we shouldn't try to make it better. Of course, no one likes to hear this, so Mavericks often end up in hot water because some in power interpret new ideas or disagreements as a challenge to their leadership. How unfortunate!

103

"The truth is, when an organization is in crisis, it will probably be a Maverick who will bail it out with an original solution. So when an organization listens to its Mavericks, it safeguards against corporate failure and ensures long-term success." Kip's emphatic tone told John that his mentor was speaking from personal experience.

John wanted to make sure he understood the Maverick. "Are Mavericks, then, the complainers—the people who play devil's advocate?"

"Not at all. They are independent thinkers who may see a different solution from the rest of the group. For them the issue isn't dissent. Because they have vision, they look to more far-reaching solutions to problems than the majority. If they have to complain or play devil's advocate, they will, but for them the only issue is getting the best results possible."

"Does that mean that we must always accept the opinion of Mavericks?"

"Of course not. Mavericks often come up with highly impractical ideas. The key is to learn to listen with an open mind before judging the merit of an idea. Furthermore, it's important to recognize how much courage it takes to be a Maverick."

"Courage? Why courage?" asked John.

"Have you ever stood up and offered an opinion at a meeting?" asked Kip.

"Sure, but I was always uncomfortable until I saw how people responded to it."

"Meaning that if your idea was liked, you relaxed again?"

John nodded.

"Now, imagine spending your life offering proposals and ideas that are frequently rejected. If you have the guts to get up again and again and propose new ideas, don't you think you would be courageous?"

"I see your point, Kip."

"All right, now that we understand the Dominant Trait of a Maverick, let's discuss the **9-to-5-er**."

John smiled a slightly disparaging smile, which did not escape Kip's notice.

"Because of the term I use for them, you might think I don't respect 9-to-5-ers," he said, eyeing John intently. "Nothing could be further from the truth. The historian Will Durant explains it best. He says the story of humankind is like a river. The major personalities and events are like torrents that sweep everything in their wake. But on the banks of the river are the villagers who live their lives, raise their families, grow their food, regardless of what Heroic or terrible events occur around them.

"Think of the 9-to-5-ers as these villagers. They are involved in building a better life for themselves and their families. While they're at work, they work. And if you give them good instructions and treat them with respect, they'll do a good job.

"But for them, work is not everything. They balance their life between work and play. They are devoted parents, and they have a strong sense of community. But if you ever need them, they'll go the extra mile for you, as long as you treat them with the respect they deserve.

106

The 9-to-5-er Has a Role, Too!

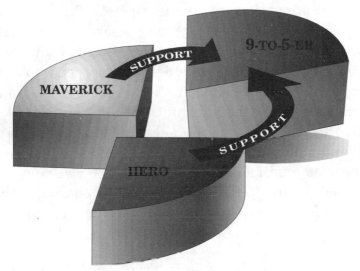

"9-to-5-ers are also the most influenced by their working environment. They can be either motivated or apathetic—it all depends on the way they are treated. It also takes courage to be a 9-to-5-er."

John wasn't convinced. "Why would you call 9-to-5-ers courageous?"

"Let me answer you with a little story. Not long ago I sat by a young woman on an airplane. Her name was Cynthia. Her company was sending her for a computer course to learn new skills in her area—inventory control. I asked her about her job and her life. She told me she was divorced with two young children. She was a devoted mother who was frustrated because she didn't always have the time she wanted for the kids, but she did her best. She also held a full-time job she had to commute for over an hour each way and in which she had just received a promotion. In addition, she was going to school one night a week. And yet here she was, willing to learn new skills to help her company do better. Now I ask you, is Cynthia courageous?"

"I see what you mean. Like the unsung Heroes of wartime, 9-to-5-ers are the unsung Heroes of the workplace," John said with a new sense of respect.

"Now you understand!" Kip said with emphasis. "9-to-5-ers may not set the world on fire with their leadership or creativity, but day in and day out, they carry on the work they are assigned. Without them the organization would sputter and come to a halt."

John remained silent for a while. He was beginning to realize that deep respect for all people is the foundation for the Heroic Environment. He remembered recent incidents where he might have been abrupt with some of his plant workers, and he felt inwardly embarrassed. He resolved to not let that happen again.

Finally, his attention returned to his conversation with Kip.

"Tell me about the last personality trait—the **Dissident.**"

"Ah, yes, the Dissident . . . he or she is an integral part of almost every organization," Kip said thoughtfully. "But before I talk about the Dissident, I'd like to make three points. First, unlike the other Dominant Traits, which are a part of people's basic makeup, Dissident behavior is often created by circumstances at the workplace. Second, this behavior is the only one of the four that is essentially negative. Third, and most important, I want to make sure you understand that Dissident Behavior is not the same as dissenting opinion. In the Heroic Environment, dissenting opinions are actively encouraged, even sought after. An honest difference of opinion is vital to the survival and success of any organization. The key to honest dissent is that the disagreement comes out of a genuine desire to help the group achieve its goals. On the other hand, Dissident Behavior, as I define it here, happens when a person no longer roots for the team's success."

"Why wouldn't someone want to see his own team win?" asked John.

"There are several reasons. A Dissident could be a former Maverick whose proposal was rejected for someone else's and who now is hoping that the accepted proposal will fail. Or he could be a 9-to-5-er who feels that his leaders are not 'walking the talk' and is therefore bitter. The Dissident could be a fallen Hero who cannot accept the authority of another leader . . . "

"I see," interrupted John. "People who no longer see themselves as *part* of the team often become the Dissidents."

"That's it in a nutshell!" said Kip, impressed with John's insight.

110

"Then what we must do as soon as we see Dissident behavior is help that person feel once again part of the team," continued John, taking over the discussion. "It all goes back to the Heroic Behavior of helping people feel like insiders, doesn't it?"

Kip nodded.

"The way I see it," John continued, "we all feel outside the team sometimes. The worst possible thing to do would be to isolate the Dissident further."

"Well done, John. You're on the right track. The best way to help Dissidents is to embrace them and bring them back on board. Of course, this doesn't always work. Ultimately, Dissidents themselves must recognize their own counterproductive behavior."

John seemed perplexed, so Kip continued.

"Let me tell you this story to illustrate what I mean.

"Two partners, Alan and Peter, who together had built an advertising agency, were at a point where their differences had begun to destroy their relationship. In the early years they were inseparable and their business had grown and prospered. They genuinely liked and enjoyed each other. Often, in the middle of a sales presentation, one would finish the other's sentence. But with the passage of time that all changed. Both men came to dwell upon the other's shortcomings, missed opportunities, blind spots, and vulnerabilities. Instead of acting Heroically and putting the other's interest first, their bickering turned ugly. In fact, they communicated with each other mostly through their administrative assistants, who nicknamed the situation 'the Cold War.'

"Alan was the older of the two and served as head copywriter for the agency. He had a sharp wit, was a natty dresser, and demanded perfection from his staff. Peter, a free spirit, was the creative art director. His suits never seemed to be pressed and his style was imprecise. But his employees and clients loved him for his spontaneity and gift for design. Each man's strengths matched the other's weaknesses.

"Because of their Cold War, the entire agency suffered. Employees were actively taking sides, with the popular Peter definitely winning the loyalty of the team. Alan was feeling increasingly isolated at his own agency.

"One day the agency was invited to present its work to a major potential client who had been on their dream list for years. Here was their big chance, and it couldn't have happened at a more critical time. Their Cold War had taken its toll, and the company was on its last legs financially. Getting this account could save their agency.

"As is sometimes the case with busy clients, they were asked to give their presentation on the weekend. Peter insisted on driving. Alan relented, uneasily, even though Peter was known to run late. The presentation was to be held in New Jersey, and Peter promised to pick Alan up at his New York City apartment at 10:30 A.M. sharp, giving them plenty of time to arrive at their noon presentation.

"Alan was downstairs at the curb ten minutes early just to make sure; 10:30 came, no Peter. By

10:45 Alan was upset. By 11:00 he was contemplating murder.

"Finally, at 11:10, Peter pulled up, completely unruffled at being forty minutes late. Alan, losing every vestige of self-control and feeling sorry for himself, started screaming at Peter, 'You've made us miss the presentation! I knew I shouldn't have trusted you! Now we'll never make it on time.'

"Peter calmly turned to Alan and said, 'Don't worry, I've got a shortcut!'

" 'A what?' shrieked Alan. 'A shortcut,' said Peter. 'In fact, that's why I'm late—I was getting the directions. This shortcut will chop nearly twenty-five minutes from the ride, so we have plenty of time.'

"As he entered the car, Alan was still bristling. For once, he wanted Peter to get his comeuppance. Suddenly, he had a realization. 'Good Heavens, what am I hoping for?' he thought. 'Am I hoping Peter's shortcut will work and get us there on time so we can get the account, or am I hoping he'll fail in order to reinforce my belief that Peter is a fool who's responsible for all our problems?'"

"What happened? Did they get to the client's place on time?" John asked eagerly.

The old man paused for a moment. "You know, I didn't know if they got there on time. What's important here is Alan's moment of discovery and enlightenment. He realized that what people root for is sometimes in conflict with their own best interest and the interest of the team."

John was silent. The story of Alan and Peter affected him because he could see there had been a few times when he too had not rooted for his team's success, especially when he'd felt slighted. Was he a Dissident, then? He started going over the four Dominant Traits in his mind. No, he concluded, he *couldn't* be a Dissident. The role of the Hero—helping, encouraging, championing others—clearly attracted him the most. And he remembered Kip's comments that becoming a Hero was a never-ending process. He felt he had a long way to go. Suddenly, he had new insight and with it, new questions.

"Kip, you keep talking about each of us having a *Dominant* Trait. Does this mean that we have other traits as well? As I think about my experiences, I can see that I have acted in all four capacities at one time or another."

"You know, John, you have great deal of insight for someone so young," Kip responded respectfully. "You are right, of course. No one's behavior is one-dimensional. In fact, have you ever noticed how many roles you play in a day? For example, when you return routine phone calls, you may be acting like any of thousands of 9-to-5-ers. An hour later you may be backing a new proposal presented by an unpopular person solely because you see its merit. At that moment you are acting like a Hero."

I see what you mean. During one work day I may be changing roles several times, using different traits."

"Right. And yet, for each of us there is a Dominant Trait that defines our personality most of the time. But as the situation dictates, each of us may switch roles."

John nodded in understanding, but he wasn't yet satisfied. "Kip, we talked about Dissidents, and we agree that they should be made to feel part of the team again, or that they need to have an insight into their own behavior. But what happens if, as happened to me, you have an employee who is so bent on the righteousness of his cause that he deliberately sabotages the organization's efforts?"

"Then you may have on your hands a more complex and dangerous situation," Kip answered gravely. "You may have encountered the type I call the **Terrorist.**"

John's eyes widened as Kip continued in a low voice. "There are some people, and they are very few, who can never see themselves as part of the team. The reasons are complex, ranging from lack of family identification as children to a sense of quiet superiority to the group. It's not a healthy psychological state."

"Are they Terrorists because they don't want to fit in?"

"No, they are Terrorists because of their behavior. For example, they may be computer programmers who introduce a faulty program—they call it

117

a *computer virus*—just to destroy the work of others. Or they may engage in industrial espionage. They rationalize their behavior by creating in their minds wrongs and injustices that don't exist."

"Are there many Terrorists in a typical organization?"

"Fortunately, Terrorists are pretty rare. But their destructive ability far exceeds their number."

John let out a low whistle.

Kip continued, "Great care must be taken before labeling someone a Terrorist. In fact, if you aren't careful with your labels you could get yourself into a heap of trouble. Only extreme behavior would ever fall into this category."

"What do you do when you're absolutely positive that someone is a Terrorist?" inquired John.

"If I were absolutely convinced that someone was acting in a way that was causing the organization definite harm, I would have to move for that person's dismissal. But again, you must be very careful to document your case with facts and not suspicions."

"Kip, you seem so careful in talking about Terrorist behavior. Why?"

"Because too often in autocratic organizations people use labels to unjustly crucify their enemies. If I'm reluctant to talk about this issue it's because I'm sensitive to the injustice people suffered because of their background or politics. Even in America we had to deal with the McCarthy era hysteria. People in an organization can also get paranoid and start labeling anyone who disagrees with the authorities as Terrorists. So please, be careful with this," Kip concluded emphatically.

John looked at his watch. It was almost 10:30.

"We'll be in Kansas City soon," Kip said with barely disguised excitement.

It took a moment before John remembered that Kansas City was where he was to meet Peggy

Bentley, Kip's goddaughter and the California Zephyr's chief engineer for the next shift.

♦ ♦ ♦

The train screeched to a halt, and the loudspeaker blared their arrival in Kansas City. Kip turned to John. "Better take your overcoat if you'd like to join me. We'll have to get off the train and walk to the front to reach the engineer's compartment."

John inhaled the bracing air as they exited their car. It felt good, although the contrast to his warm compartment was a shock to his senses. The terminal was unusually busy for that time of night, with lots of sleepy children in the arms of their parents. John followed Kip, who was walking briskly through the scattered crowds. In spite of his years, Kip had the buoyant gait of someone half his age.

When they finally reached the engine, Kip called to Peggy, who was just about to embark. They greeted each other affectionately.

John waited for the two to catch up on family news. Shortly after, Kip turned around and introduced them to each other.

Peggy was an energetic woman in her mid-thirties, with intelligent eyes and a friendly yet professional manner. As she shook hands with John, Kip recounted to Peggy the topic of their conversation.

Peggy smiled a smile of recognition. "So what do you think of the Heroic Environment?"

"I think it's the most important concept I've ever heard," John replied quietly but firmly.

Peggy's face turned serious. "Well, they certainly don't teach these kinds of ideas in school. But I know they work."

"How?" asked John.

"Because Kip helped my father institute the concepts in his business, and they have been a guiding light for him and, incidentally, for our entire family ever since."

"What made you decide to become a railroad engineer . . . I mean, it's not the typical career. . . ."

"You mean for a woman, don't you?" Peggy said, laughing. "I'm afraid Kip is responsible for that, too. I've always loved trains, and Kip encouraged me to pursue my dream, even though it was unconventional."

"So now that you've achieved your goal . . ."

"I haven't achieved my goal," interrupted Peggy. "My goal is to bring back rail travel as a major way of transporting people. We're a long way from that, and yet our highways are becoming more and more crowded and our air more polluted. But I'm gratified to see how many people are coming back to train travel. One day, I hope we'll use it here as much as it is used in other developed countries like Japan, France, and Germany."

"And how do you propose to achieve this?" John asked, fascinated.

"I want to keep reinforcing the progress we're making by helping institute the Heroic Environment here. And to do this properly, I hope one day to become a leader and spokesperson for the rail industry."

"Wow, you certainly know what you want," John said, a bit enviously.

"Don't you, John?"

"I'm still working on it," confided the young man, suddenly feeling like a high school freshman.

Kip, who had been listening to the exchange with keen interest, jumped in. "I have no doubts that John will make important contributions. But for now, we all must board the train."

For the first time, John noticed that he was tired. It had been a long and exciting day. After saying their goodbyes to Peggy, Kip and John returned to their compartment. Their bunks had been turned down for the night. Both agreed to continue their discussion in the morning.

Chapter 6

Telling Someone You Like That You Are Sorry

As the train picked up speed leaving the Kansas City Station, John knew that his day of learning was just about over. But deep in his heart, he still had one unanswered question. It kept creeping back into his mind, and he knew that unless he got the answer, he would be enjoying an unwelcomed sleeping companion—*his conscience*. John decided to request one more insight from his mentor before he turned in for the night.

"Kip, I've been thinking about a situation I have facing me when I return to work on Monday, and it's been bothering me," said John.

Kip turned toward John slowly. He realized that the young man was carrying some trouble around in his pocket, and the weight was taking its toll. "John, it sounds important, so why don't you tell me about it and let's see if we can figure out what to do?"

John took a deep breath and began. "Kip, it started late last year. I was introduced to the head of another department at work that had been producing parts similar to our division. This fellow and I hit it off right away. I guess you could say that we had a lot of the same values. But early on, something went haywire. In looking back at the situation, I guess I appeared stubborn and assertive about my position and ideas. As you already know, I'm not afraid to speak my mind and to stand up for what I believe. Sometimes it is a little much for those around me. And in this case, it was about how an existing product could be built *better* and what features it would offer.

"The other fellow had been building a similar product for years and was rightfully proud of his techniques and experience. From my perspective, I expected him to come over to my way of thinking and tried to communicate that belief. In our last get-together, I really blew it. We were supposed to work on a joint project, but the fellow felt so put off by my approach that I received a letter from him the next day expressing his frustration, anger, and hurt feelings. He even went so far as to terminate our joint project."

Kip could see that John was feeling as bad as the other fellow. Carefully, Kip broke the silence after John's confession, and began in a slow and deliberate manner to help John sort through his dilemma. "Whew! It sounds like the other fellow is pretty upset with you. For whatever it's worth, I believe the other fellow is feeling the same hurt, frustration, and embarrassment, and also might want to smooth out the situation. But first, let's step back from the sparks and concentrate on the substance of your comments and the disagreement. What did you say that caused such a reaction, and how did you act?" asked Kip with compassion. Kip had a unique way of getting to the heart of a situation without making the other person defensive.

John appreciated the opportunity to openly discuss his comments and feelings. "Kip, I've gone over and over the conversation in my mind these past several weeks. I believed I had told the truth as I saw it, but it sure didn't come across that way."

"Maybe it was the truth. But I suspect it was more like *your* truth," said Kip, smiling. "Sometimes our personal truths, beliefs, or convictions aren't someone else's, and that is generally where the trouble begins. As we try harder and harder to convince the other person, the effect is exactly the opposite of what we want.

"John, do you remember the 'Peter and Alan' story? Well, I never told you what happened."

"I know," said John.

"These men had been close friends. They had admired each other. Now they loathed each other. And this had come about because of their communications, not because of their Shared Values."

"I know, but these things happen, don't they?" asked John, somewhat perplexed.

"John, during the trip to New Jersey something magical happened. Here were two men, who had been architects of the 'Cold War' at the agency, and they were pulling together as a team to get to the presentation on time. All the petty fighting and snide attacks between them were gone. They were just two guys weaving their way through Saturday traffic, working together for a common cause. Sometimes that's all it takes to create a defining moment."

John understood what Kip was offering him— an approach to patch things up.

"The breakthrough began after Alan realized that what he was rooting for was important. This not only turned the day into a success, but started the transition from a no-win situation involving enormous hurt feelings, deep anger, and frustration, into the beginning steps of rekindling the friendship between Peter and Alan. Alan turned to Peter and said 'This is great. We are working together again. I guess we need to stop trying to convince each other of anything and instead focus on the areas of interest we have in common.' Alan had stated the obvious, of course, but this breakthrough statement was the defining moment for the two men.

"By the time they reached the presentation site, the 'Berlin Wall' between them was coming down."

"I guess even the client saw the difference?" asked John.

"You bet the client saw the difference. It was this difference which turned their luck around. In fact, Peter and Alan received the nod to begin in earnest the development of a three-million-dollar-ad campaign. Not all stories end with a happy ending. Luckily, this one did.

"John, here were two men who had a lot in common. Their intentions were good, they each recognized the other's talents, but they were forgetting one very important thing: Respecting another person's ideas and contributions requires extraordinary caring and commitment. The Heroic act of *putting the interest of others first* applies here. John, sometimes in our enthusiasm to convince, we say things that *diminish* the other person's *trust* in us.

"Further, we are ignoring the other person's need for *personal autonomy, significance,* and *ac-*

132

ceptance. And when we forget these needs, it leads to what you described as the other fellow's frustration, anger, and hurt feelings."

Kip had done a little unloading on John and wanted to make sure that his young companion was receiving the information in the way in which it was intended. "John, how does this sync with what might have happened?"

John had listened intently to Kip's explanation. "I guess I wasn't acting Heroically, was I?"

"John, I can't say. But it sure seems like you could get a second chance. Remember that you said he wrote you a note? Well, from my experience, when a person takes the time to write a note, he is quietly hoping that a crack in the door will offer a future opportunity to mend the fence.

"Perhaps, with this passage of time, now is the right moment to try. I'd say that you might consider moderating your energy while trying to convince the other person, and focus on the areas that you agree on. I believe that's good advice for us all. What do you think?"

John realized that he now had enough insight and information to try to repair the damage. After all, he liked and respected the other fellow, and he had looked forward to their becoming fast friends. Instead, he had forgotten some truths about how to treat another person. He was convinced that it was worth the effort and looked forward to extending the olive branch as soon as he got back to the office.

"Kip, thanks for listening. I really needed to sort that out before I called it a night."

"John, we all run into walls ... myself included. What I hope you know is that people are rooting for you, and I know that deep down you are pulling for them."

It had been a long day. John would sleep well.

Chapter 7

The Mystery of Organizational Success

John woke up at 5:58 A.M., just two minutes before his alarm was set to go off. As he reached to
intercept its ring, he started to sit up and saw Kip
sitting on his bunk reading, already shaved and
dressed.

"Good morning," John said, as he got himself
into a sitting position.

"Morning," replied Kip smiling. "Did you sleep
well?"

"Yes I did, thanks. Did you?"

"Well, I don't need quite as much sleep as I used to. I usually get up around 4:00 A.M. and take a walk. Sometimes I go back to bed, and sometimes I don't."

"I'm glad you're awake, Kip. Last night you began talking about the four behavior styles, but I have some more questions before I can really understand the role these different styles play in an organization. Give me a couple of minutes to wash up and get dressed."

Upon John's return, the two men began talking.

"Let me continue our discussion about these four individual styles by saying that they are *all* necessary in a Heroic organization," said Kip. "For years I enthusiastically searched for what I came to call the *mystery of organizational success.*"

"Why is it a mystery?" asked the young man.

"Well, John, because if the four dominant styles—the Hero, the Maverick, the 9-to-5-er, and the Dissident—aren't in place, you can't have a true Heroic Environment." Kip took another sheet of paper from his briefcase and drew a pie-shaped graph that showed how the four styles relate to each other.

"You see, only when an organization has all four personality types working as a unit will it reach its potential. These four styles act as a balanced system, which allows an organization to recognize change and creatively respond to opportunities," said Kip enthusiastically.

"What happens if the four styles aren't found in an organization?" asked John.

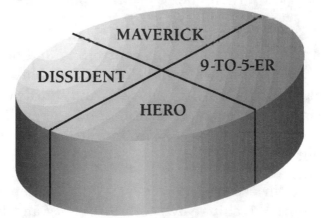

"Then it is vulnerable and brittle. This inflexibility causes major blind spots, and its bout with disaster is only a matter of time," said the older man.

"A Hero who isn't occasionally challenged by a Dissident will lose his humility and blunder. A Maverick who is not championed by a Hero will become frustrated. A 9-to-5-er who isn't inspired by a Hero will lose enthusiasm. Heroes and Mavericks who are not supported by 9-to-5-ers will lose time and effectiveness."

John realized the truth of what he was hearing. "It all works together so naturally, it seems. But suppose you have an organization that has an autocratic environment. What happens then?"

"Simply stated, organizations that are autocratic—those I refer to as controlling and bossy—tend to scare away the Heroes and Mavericks. That is why really talented and hardworking people fail in one organization and succeed in another." Kip then drew what an autocratic environment would look like.

"So, in essence, 9-to-5-ers and Dissidents are running the ship. Now, both 9-to-5-ers and Dissi-

An Autocratic Environment

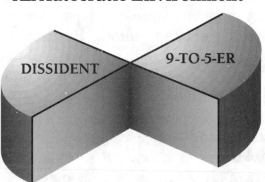

dents are important, but they can't carry the full load without help. Help comes in the form of Heroes. Heroes facilitate the Mavericks, who generate ideas."

"So, Heroes and Mavericks are the most important types," said John.

"No, all four styles are important. The key is balance," said the older man.

"Well, is there ever a time when you can't find Heroes and Mavericks, even when the environment would be responsive to them?" asked John.

Kip replied, "Because everyone can be a Hero at the right moment, you don't have to worry about never having enough Heroes. By simply creating an environment that is Heroic, you will never have a shortage. The secret or mystery is in understanding the need for a balance of these four styles."

"I understand that a balance of the four dominant styles is necessary, but wouldn't it be better to get rid of all Dissidents?" asked John.

"First, all of us have a Dissident behavior style lying in wait. This dormant behavior only comes out when we are not rooting for a successful outcome. Remember, a contrary point of view is *not* Dissident behavior. Some managers and people in authority have used the term Dissident for years to describe anyone who doesn't agree with their opinion. This is why the term has become confusing.

"This style keeps everyone honest. Dissidents are like investigative reporters. Their role is important because they help companies strengthen their stance before acting out of unchallenged false confidence. Dissidents don't go to management with their complaints, but they do go to the 9-to-5-ers. In a Heroic Environment, a process is established for hearing the Dissidents' ideas," said Kip.

Kip realized that they hadn't eaten yet, and suggested that they would be wise to grab a seat in the dining car before it got too crowded.

"I agree. I'm starving!" said John.

As the two men walked back to the dining car, John began to understand in more detail why a balance of the four styles was critical to the success and survival of an organization.

Chapter 8

The Curse of Conditional Thinking

The morning sun had broken cleanly through the high clouds as the train sped toward its next stop. Some of the passengers would be leaving the train to visit their families. John still had a long way to go, not in miles, but in his understanding. He knew that he would have Kip's company for only a little while longer, and he wanted to make every minute count.

As they entered the dining car, John turned and said, "Kip, I have a serious question to figure out. You know, sometimes I realize that I wish some of the people around me would change."

"What do you mean, 'change'?" asked Kip as he glided into his window seat.

"What I really mean to say is that some of the things people say or do bug me or get me downright angry and frustrated!"

"And what do you generally do about it?" asked Kip intently, looking John straight in the eye.

John thought that Kip's question was a little off the point. After all, if he knew what to do, why would he have asked Kip in the first place? But John knew that Kip generally didn't ask a question if he didn't already have a pretty good idea of what the answer was or should be.

"Kip, I get angry and stew about it mostly. It's just so difficult to say what is on my mind. You know, sometimes I think my emotions get in the way of thinking clearly at such a moment. Is that hard to understand?"

"Not at all. Frankly, it took me quite a few years to understand that emotions often block our most productive thoughts. And they sometimes even put us on the wrong trail in terms of finding solutions to our interpersonal dilemmas. Let me see if I can explain what I mean.

"All of us, as we 'walk our talk,' begin to have a sense of what is okay. Think of it this way: Unknowingly, we begin to develop a gigantic set of lists. Now, these lists identify *everything* we do, and everything *everyone else* does. Not only do we develop our own lists, but we are careful to make sure that our internal *rating* system values every item on the list.

"Now, because it is our list and our rating system, we are pretty sure of being right about our opinions and impressions. I bet you've heard the expression, 'That's what makes a horse race.'"

John was puzzled. "What does it mean?"

"Well, when I was a young man, I couldn't understand why some people wore one type of hat, and other people wore many different hats. I remember my mother saying, 'That's what makes a horse race.'

149

"I think she was suggesting that if everyone wore the same hat, or bet on the same horse, it would be a pretty dull world. John, people see the world differently, and that's the beauty of it all. There's no way we are all going to vote for the same candidate or practice the same religion. People innately want to be able to choose. The French say, 'Vive la différence!'

"But the truth is, even though people see things differently, we don't usually give them credit for their choices, especially if their choices seem strange or out of step with our idea of the way things should be. Unless we take control of it, this is where our 'rating system' starts to get us in trouble. Left unchecked, it could lead us to become narrow-minded, or worse."

John could now see where Kip was going with his story. Kip was gently suggesting that John's *rating system* was getting in the way of John's giving other people their rightful place in the spotlight. John's frustration and impatience with other people's behavior were leading him to judge people according to his standards of how the world was "supposed" to be.

"I never thought of having an internal rating system, but now that you bring it up, I do have standards and beliefs. Maybe I do judge others by my standards, but what is so wrong with that?" asked John. "Doesn't everyone?"

"Of course they do," said Kip emphatically. "And that is what starts to cause some pretty interesting dilemmas. Not only do we have an internal rating system, but so does everyone else.

"And to complicate this, we each compare our rating system with theirs. Each of our rating systems gets modified somewhat when we realize that we need to 'compare notes'—then we have a chance to sort out our differences."

"I know it is better to get your differences out in the open, but I don't always do that," said John.

"John, give yourself some slack. Believe me, no one ever does. But when we don't do it, we begin to go down the path of what I call *conditional thinking*."

"What in the heck is *conditional thinking*?" asked John.

"John, conditional thinking is when we place conditions of acceptance and support on those around us. Let me explain by giving you an example.

"Let's say that you are working with someone over an extended period of time, and you begin to know more about his or her x's and o's than you did when you first met that person. x's and o's are the pluses and minuses that we all have. Over time, we begin to learn about people we work with, and their x's and o's start to show up in living color. John, everyone has them. Even me, I'm afraid to say. If we began to work with each other, day in and day out, we'd learn plenty about each other."

"Yeah, and you'd learn about my x's pretty darned fast!" said John, half-smiling.

"Well, John, it isn't the fact that you have your faults that matters—it's how the rest of us think about your faults that really counts," said Kip. "During my many years of working with people, I have come to understand a critical step.

"Many of us learn to cope with others' faults by conditionally supporting these people. We begin to justify in our own minds that we can no longer fully support them. But, because we need to continue to work with them, we begin to modify our unconditional support and attach percentage points to our feelings about them and their faults. You'll always know if conditional support is occurring when you hear people say, 'I can't support you 100 percent on that' or '70 percent of the time I support you, but the other 30 percent of the time I must take exception to your ways.'"

"What's so bad about that approach?" asked John.

"Just about everything!" said Kip. "When we start to put conditions on our support of other people, we are drawing the blueprint for destroying the one special element that binds us together: Our *unconditional* support for another person. Sure, there can be dozens of areas of disagreement between people; that's normal. It's when we start qualifying our support that tragedy always strikes.

"Here are some examples of how dangerous conditional support and conditional thinking are:

Imagine if in international politics we heard: *'I can only support the treaty and my defense commitments 70 percent of the time.'* Or in a marriage, if one partner said, *'I'm only faithful 80 percent of the time.'*

"How about in living by a labor contract? *'I adhere to the contract 90 percent of the time.'* In driving a car: *'I abide by the rules of the road 70 percent of the time.'*

"John, you can see how dangerous this conditional approach can be. And, oh yes, conditional support and thinking are *never* really satisfied. The moment one condition is met, something always comes up that sets off the discontent all over again."

"Gee, Kip, I never looked at it that way. But what is the alternative?"

"John, I'm glad you asked. The easiest way to answer your question is to ask you a question in return. If you were to live your life devoid of conditional thinking, how would you do it?"

"That's simple," said John. "I'd give people my full support! And I wouldn't place conditions on my commitment to them."

"Bravo, John!" said Kip. "It really is as simple as that. And you will know that you have gotten rid of conditional thinking when the snide comments, backdoor conversations, second-guessing, and critical expressions start disappearing from *your* behavior.

"John, in a Heroic Environment, sarcasm and side conversations begin to disappear. And, when this happens, our personal internal lists and rating systems—of what's acceptable and what's not—also disappear."

John had a puzzled look on his face. "But what about all the differences I have with other people? You know, some of the people I work with are pretty frustrating."

"John, the best advice I can give you is to throw away your bloody forms and checklists and start talking out your differences. Here are five quick guidelines for building an approach to remove conditional thinking from your life:

"Number One: Approach the other person within twenty-four hours. We call it the Twenty-Four-Hour rule.

"Number Two: Ask the other person if this is a good time to communicate. In fact, I suggest you always use the same phrase when you approach the other person. I say, 'Is this a good time to talk?' And then I wait for their response. Make sure that if the other person says it's not a good time to talk, you schedule a better time. We call this rule the Joan Rivers rule."

"Yeah, I know, 'Can We Talk?'" Both men smiled. "What's rule number three?"

"Number Three: Make sure you approach the other person in a nonthreatening fashion. Only the other person can truly determine whether you are successful with this. It will take practice to be able to read their reactions and tell when you are coming across in a threatening manner.

"Number Four: We suggest when you have your conversation with the other person that you talk straight without hurting the other person's feelings. Keep your language simple, understandable, and, above all, nonapologetic, and nonpersonal. And finally . . .

"Number Five: Make sure that you make requests of the other person, and don't give him or her complaints or opinions. I'd also go one step further and tell the other person how you'd like things to be. Don't demand anything—just make a straightforward, respectful request."

John was writing on his napkin as fast as he could. "Kip, these five guidelines seem as though they could be used at home as well as at work."

"You bet they can. In fact, I'd teach them to everyone. After all, if they work for you, they should and do work for everyone."

"Kip, these seem like a set of standards. Are they the standards for any of the eight Heroic principles?"

"So, you picked up on that, did you? Yes, John, these five steps are the standards for treating others with uncompromising truth. How do you like these guidelines?"

John could only smile and nod. "I love them. I can use these immediately and begin to rid myself of conditional thinking, and make a real change in the way I communicate and make my thoughts and feelings known."

Kip was pleased with John's response. "Now, I caution you to make sure that your differences are fundamental to moving your organization forward, and that your differences do not stem from your personal ideas on how things should be. Remember, we all have our own style of doing things. Some of us are pretty private by nature, others of us talk in a slow and deliberate way, some of us look at a situation from every angle, and others of us are enthusiastic and promoting.

"Some of us like to wear our hair long, while others of us like to wear our hair short. All personality types, like our Heroes, Mavericks, 9-to-5-ers, and Dissidents, are found in every organization and must be respected and defended for their differences and their personal expression.

"These differences are at the heart of every team's strength. Cut out or shun one of these personalities, and your organization will not have the depth necessary to grow and change rapidly.

"John, one more thing. I believe that politicking your point of view is always destructive and counterproductive in the final analysis. Talking with another individual to shore up your collective values and shared goals is important and fundamental in sustaining a long-lasting relationship.

"Seeking group support for your ideas or point of view before you go to the person you are in conflict with causes future misunderstandings and adds to the negative political nature of an organization. Not only does it undermine the other person, but it does nothing for your credibility. Remember, to everyone else you come across as someone who may also be talking about them.

"John, George Washington said, 'One man makes a majority.' Be confident in your judgment.

It takes practice, but it is worth taking the risk for the organization's sake. Stop going around testing the water to see if others agree with your point of view."

In a few short moments, John had gained an invaluable insight into how to be free from the trap of conditional thinking. It was a lesson that he would need to practice when he got home to Denver, and he was eager to begin.

Chapter 9

The Role of the Navigator in a Heroic Environment

As soon as they were back in their compartment, John looked at Kip thoughtfully. John was excited about this morning's breakfast conversation, because he could now use Kip's guidelines with his family as well as his co-workers.

Although he loved his wife very much, he could see how his conditional thinking was affecting their relationship. Even his thoughts about his daughter, Lauren, were colored by his conditional thinking. He knew he would be seeing his family in less than two hours, and he could hardly wait.

With the information Kip had given him, John knew he could now make intelligent, thoughtful decisions about his career and readjust his approach to the people he loved. He was now armed with important insights into how people really wanted to be treated and thought about.

While Kip was arranging his books, John asked, "Kip, before our journey together ends, are there any other important areas we should cover?"

"Let's talk about change," said Kip. "Perhaps one of the most important things to understand is the tremendous speed at which change occurs today. This is especially true in business, where economic conditions, technological breakthroughs, and consumer preferences can unearth new opportunities or cause loss of business almost overnight.

"The problem is that most organizations aren't set up to respond quickly enough to change."

"I'm sure you are right," said John. "But there are a lot of old-style, autocratic companies that keep making a profit year after year. It's hard to argue for a change when their stock keeps going up."

"Not really," said Kip. "Here are some statistics which might interest you. By 1970, more than half of the Fortune 500 companies of 1950 were eaten up by mergers or closed for lack of profitability. In fact, by the middle of the 1980s, few of these companies remained in business under their original name, or with the descendants of their original management group.

"By the turn of the twenty-first century, the entire manufacturing and service industries will have been reinvented. At least half of the people who had a particular job in 1985 will have a new one requiring new skills by this century's end. Companies that will lead every nation's economy are forming as we speak, and the ones we currently know may not make it into the next century. There are no lifetime job guarantees anymore, even for model workers and managers. Now, there's a lot of change facing everyone!"

"What can we do about this?" asked John.

"There are many things we can do about it. One thing some people are doing about it is putting their heads in the sand. Not a great solution long-term, but in the short-term it might work." Both Kip and John shook their heads and furled their lips in mock amusement.

Getting serious again, Kip continued, "The common thread to the organizations in the most danger is that they do not have a strategy or culture which accepts change with enthusiasm.

"John, the reason most companies disappear is that they lack the process to accept and benefit from new information and to make the appropriate course-of-action corrections. *If you think any company is immune from this disease, you're wrong.* Even the 'biggest' or 'bluest' aren't immune." John knew exactly which organizations Kip was singling out.

"Even government and the educational system in our country need to heed this warning. Nothing is forever. Any organization which forgets that it is in service to its customers, and must meet their needs, is a target for extinction. Once an organization loses sight of this fact, it is headed for the scrap heap.

"John, without the ability to see the future, organizations tragically lose their way. In most instances, a safe passage is not clearly marked, and it requires sharp navigators and able communicators to find the way."

"I bet you are going to say that each company that is to survive listens to its employees and is able to effectively interpret its Business and People Values," said John.

Kip smiled the smile of one who knows that his mentoring is taking hold. "Not only will they survive, but many will become the world leaders in their field. Often the Navigators are not the senior managers of an organization. In the old days, we expected top management to have the vision. In the future, we will need everyone's help to see the true path. No longer will tradition forecast our future. Past reputations, successes, and even lessons will not be enough to survive and prosper. A new partnership must be developed between management and the employees of an organization. You might consider it a new communication and philosophical contract between the two groups.

"In the future, the organizations which ignore and shun this vital partnership between the Navigators and management will fail. This *must* not happen."

"Why are these Navigators so important? Isn't it the role of management to anticipate change?" asked the young man.

"John, Navigators are crucial to organizations which seek a future. Reading danger signals and conveying advance information, making choices and heeding warnings will never be more important than they will be in the next ten years," answered Kip.

"The companies that disappear will have leaders who maintained old, autocratic, controlling tactics. Centralizing strategies will become a noose around many organizations' throats. 'Fast and lean' will become the order of the day. Right now, organizations are consolidating and merging, but in the future the advantage will go to those companies who choose to share responsibility, and vital market and financial information, with their people. If an organization wants to know about its one Achilles heel—which will do it in in times of trouble—it needs to address the phenomenon which I call *filtered information!*"

"What is *filtered information?*" asked John.

"*Filtered information* is information that has been screened before it is sent upstairs. Think of it this way: Let's suppose you saw a trend that you felt could adversely affect the future of the company, but you also knew that this information went against the beliefs of the CEO and, more than likely, would be immediately rejected and could even put your career at risk. Would you send it upstairs?" asked Kip.

"You bet I wouldn't! Or, at least I would word it so that *it* and *I* might have a chance to survive," said John, knowing he probably was making the right political choice, but not stating what he would really like to do if his job wasn't on the line.

Kip immediately jumped on his words. "Then, you'd be sending filtered information upstairs, instead of sending the strong medicine needed for your senior managers to assess the situation correctly, and make the necessary changes.

"Remember, your leaders believe they are receiving fresh, unfettered information, *not* filtered information. They believe with certainty that they are considering the most current data. If they are using filtered information, they will be wrong. And their decisions will be wrong!

"Autocratic environments which view the very existence of contrary and dissenting information as threatening and destabilizing are brittle and unable to perceive change quickly, if at all. And because these organizations create a culture that is threatening to people, the only information they receive is filtered. As a result, they lose the competitive edge they need to survive and succeed." Kip continued, "And they don't even know the true cause of their vulnerability."

"Don't they recognize the danger of receiving filtered information and facilitating poor communications?" asked John.

"Yes, they would see the danger if they realized the incoming information was screened. But because they expect to see continuously confirming

170

data, and not contradictory data, they feel comfortable," said the older man.

"I think I know what you are getting at," said John. "They don't receive a different point of view, and so they believe they are on the right track."

"The more the Navigators plead for attention, the more shunned they become," Kip said. *"You know, in modern organizations we don't burn witches. We simply don't keep people around who see differently than we do."*

John said, "I believe the operative words are, 'He doesn't seem to have the right style.'"

"Yes, that is the idea." Kip continued, "Organizational discipline is the glue that holds autocratic and controlling businesses together. Their leaders' powers are tied up in their belief systems. These strong beliefs create a thick stone wall and unknowingly filter out vital information about changing market forces."

"I understand that information needs to be shared, that people at all levels of an organization have good ideas that must be heard, and that sometimes these opinions are dissenting, but not coming from a Dissident," said John. "But what is management's new leadership role?"

Kip responded quickly. "Management thinks its ultimate challenge is to *see* change. Unfortunately, you cannot plan to see change. If it were that simple, everyone would institute such a policy. Yet, when management selects a small group of senior people, including themselves, to take on this task, they usually fail."

"Then what is their most important role?" asked John.

Kip smiled. "Management's ultimate role is to create the *conditions* for seeing and responding to change and opportunities. It is their vital role to allow staff, customers, and the market to show the organization the way.

"I'm not suggesting that management take either a passive or backseat position, but that their emphasis be to establish full participation as a standard within their organization.

"Management must encourage full leadership at every level. I call this approach the establishment of a new 'citizenship' within an organization.

"In a Heroic Environment, it is essential that everyone is involved in finding solutions, not only in defining problems. You see, you and I and every other human being share something called *perceptual bias.*"

"Wait a minute," said John, "you just threw a fifty-dollar word at me!"

Kip smiled. "I'm sorry. Let me explain the meaning of *perceptual bias.* People usually see what they expect to see and ignore what they don't expect to see. This is a perceptual bias."

"You mean like not seeing your car keys that are right under your nose?" asked John.

"That is exactly it, but sometimes the consequences are a lot more dramatic," said Kip.

"Perceptual biases are frightening because we don't know we have them. They're *invisible* to us, but their effects are not! *Management's best strategy is to create a responsive environment that encourages employees to come up with innovative approaches to solving problems, rather than trying to see all the changes themselves.* With this method, senior managers reduce stress on themselves and remain responsible for the overall results.

"The combination of self-management and personal responsibility provides the best opportunity for an organization to see change and respond to changing world markets and international competition. John, think of it as *upward coaching.*

"I'm not a fortune-teller, but I'll bet that soon you'll see more and more 'good news business stories' about companies in every industry which encourage self-management and increased personal responsibility starting with their 'lowest' level employees. Opening the books and raising the shades about how operations work is a simple, but not easy, approach to success. But it is essential that every organization move in this direction if it is to survive.

"I'm afraid the alternative to this approach is a terminal case of going-out-of-business. Those businesses that hand over the company keys to their employees will dramatically increase trust at all levels within their organization!" said Kip.

"That is pretty tough stuff," remarked John. "I guess Harry Truman said it best: 'If you can't stand the heat, get out of the kitchen.' I think I like the kitchen, especially if it's in a Heroic Environment."

The two men grinned.

John took the lead in wrapping up the lesson that Kip had shared. "Let me see if I understand what you just said:

- Heroic Environments create a bond by which all people within an organization participate fully in its shared purpose, and they do this by creating a common language of values and standards.

- A company can ensure its survival and success by understanding that market forces will continue to change, and that it is up to the Navigators—at all levels of the organization—to make sure that *unfiltered* information continues to be communicated upstairs as well as downstairs, no matter how difficult it is to hear.

- With the right environment in place, companies are able to take advantage of new ideas that will spontaneously spring from any and all corners."

"You are really catching on," said Kip. "Wise managers know that all employees need to become *insiders* within their organization in order to help manage the challenging activity of seeing change."

After a slight pause, he continued. "Organizations that understand the importance of receiving unfiltered information, encouraging different opinions, applauding fresh approaches, and continuing to look for the important content without being blinded by the style of its delivery, will prosper far into the next century."

"I think I now understand what you mean about needing Navigators at *all* levels within an organization. I guess you could say that *everybody* within an organization needs to put on the hat of the Navigator," said John.

The morning skyline of Denver was just a few bends around the tracks. This new journey John was on was not ending, but just beginning.

Chapter 10

Keep Your Tracking Motor Running

Kip broke in on John's silence with an additional thought about the role of the navigator. "I'd like to help you understand how important this concept of navigation is by telling you about something that happened not too long ago." John settled back in his seat, welcoming these final remarks before he reached Denver.

Kip started slowly. "Sometimes commonsense stories are good tools to use in explaining complicated actions and events.

"A fellow was traveling for a good-sized company. In one of the cities he frequented was a hotel with a shop that sold interesting hobby and collector items. One of the items in the window was a telescope. The man decided to find out more about it. In the process, he learned a valuable lesson. He did not recognize it as such until later, when he was looking into why so few organizations continued to prosper as their market forces changed."

"Could that man have been you?" asked John.

Kip smiled and went on. "The store clerk's hobby was astronomy, and he knew a great deal about telescopes. The customer was in luck, for he received a professional presentation. At the end of the sales talk, the clerk inquired as to what the man's choice would be for a motor drive attachment."

"A what?" asked John.

"The salesman referred to the motor drive attachment as a *tracking motor*," explained Kip. "The salesman asked if the man would be using the telescope to photograph stars and constellations, and when the customer said 'yes,' the salesman suggested that he look at two 5- × 7-inch pictures.

"The first, taken without a tracking motor attached, was streaked in a very interesting way. The first contact point had some clarity. However, as the blurred line left the bright point, it faded and trailed off."

"What did the other picture look like?" asked John.

"The other picture, which was taken with a tracking motor attached, was crystal clear and seemed as though it had come from a magazine," Kip continued.

"The salesman explained that the earth, planets, and stars were all moving at tremendous velocities. Yet from the earth, and to the casual observer, the stars and planets seemed to be stationary. The salesman said that the facts, however, were quite different. Unless the telescope tracked the photographic subject, the outcome of a time-exposure photograph would be a series of blurred, useless lines.

"As a result of that sales presentation, the man learned a valuable lesson about business and about how to truly *see*. The lesson was simple."

"I think I know how this story ends," said John.

Kip smiled and asked John to go on.

"Here goes," said John. "If the man was going to keep the market forces of his business in focus, he had to recognize that they needed constant tracking because they were really always in motion, never resting."

"Another perfect score," said Kip. "In studying companies that survived and those that went out of business, it became clear that either the companies which went out of business did not understand the continual motion of the market forces, or they decided to ignore this basic law of business physics."

"Can you be more specific?" asked John.

"Yes, of course," said Kip. "In reviewing the mission statements created by the founders of many companies, I'm convinced that their missions were developed from a *static observation*. At first, as demonstrated by the picture taken without a tracking motor, the reason for being in business seemed relatively clear. Over time, the bright spot became an elongated blur. By that time, tradition and a well-entrenched bureaucratic hierarchy had control of these companies' helms, and this momentum continued to steer their courses."

"Oh boy, I think I may be working for a company just like the ones you are describing! What happened next?" asked John anxiously.

"By the time the leadership recognized that they were headed for the rocks, it was too late. The sad truth was that their tracking motors had not been turned on, and the leadership didn't know what was happening globally.

"To the naked eye, a sensation of speed cannot be sensed. Market forces are similar; they slowly move away from us when we look away for an instant," said Kip. He went on while John sat back, fascinated.

"Momentum may keep a business alive, but that is not a reliable substitute for accurate navigation," the older man said quietly.

John looked at Kip for an important answer. "The process can be reversed, can't it?" he asked.

"Yes, of course it can," said Kip helpfully. "All an organization has to do is recognize the value of its tracking motor's power and importance. I might add that everyone is responsible for keeping the tracking motor going."

John asked, "Is it hard to turn the tracking motor on?"

Kip answered carefully, "That is a difficult question to answer. For most organizations, it will take anywhere from two to five years."

"How would an organization begin?" asked John.

"Simple: Start using the Eight Principles of a Heroic Environment," said the older man with some fire in his eyes.

"You mean if organizations start treating people like they want to be treated and they *walk the talk*, the tracking motor kicks in?" exclaimed John.

Kip nodded affirmatively.

John was puzzled. "Why does it take so long to create the Heroic Environment?"

"When the majority of people within an organization understand the principles of the Heroic Environment, take responsibility for the success of their company, and work for a favorable outcome, the tracking motor will start working.

"It takes a long time for it to 'kick in' because you first have to let go of the old comfortable beliefs that make you feel safe. Then you need to learn and practice Heroic behavior.

"Heroic behavior is *not* a *program*. It is a *philosophy*. Think of it as an *operating system* which sits at the base of all the applications within your business," said Kip.

"You mean like a piece of software?" asked John.

"Well, yes and no, John. Yes, in the sense that a piece of software can be introduced into your *computer*. But we are really talking about the operating system of your *organization*, not that of a computer.

"John, the operating system of your machine touches every element. It is at the heart of the operation. If the operating system makes you efficient and intuitive in working with the other software or applications that you have running, then we would call the operating system 'user-friendly.' But this is *not* a discussion about software. The operating system I'm talking about is called the **Shared Values Process™ Operating System.** This operating system is 'people-friendly,' and you don't install it with software disks. Sorry, but it's not that easy," said Kip, with a smile.

"I understand, Kip. The operating system you're talking about has to do with using both Business Values and People Values in balance. In addition, I'd guess that it would contain standards around both the organization's Business and People Values. Kip, could I call it a *People Operating System?*" asked John.

"You certainly can," said Kip. "Remember, every organization has an operating system. It just may not have one which is in balance, or even under its control.

"Most organizations take a tactical approach to their operation, which is a short-term and short-sighted plan. Value-based operations see the long-term picture, and they base their decisions on their Business and People Values," said Kip.

"Now I understand why it will take a long-term commitment on *everyone's* part," said John.

"The key is to keep the tracking motor going," said Kip, with great seriousness. "I've seen many organizations which professed Heroic values but weren't able to sustain them because they didn't have enough navigators supporting the critical areas of the operation.

"The real power and benefit of having an operating system in place is to keep the tracking motor running smoothly so that the organization can quickly respond to opportunities, challenges, and change."

John now had the "big picture" of Kip's vision, and felt more confident about what he needed to do, but John knew he would need help from his co-workers to create the operating system Kip spoke about.

John was sure that most of his co-workers wanted the same things he did. After all, the Eight Principles of a Heroic Environment would be the best starting point he could imagine.

He could hardly wait to get started.

Chapter 11

The Beginning of a New Journey

Kip looked at his watch and said, "We'll be arriving in Denver in forty minutes." John didn't answer. He was still torn between his great desire to see his family and regret that he was about to say goodbye to his mentor.

Suddenly, he realized that he hadn't asked Kip enough questions about himself. In a way, it all seemed so mysterious. Yet John felt a genuine sense of satisfaction about the mystery. It was as if the bond between them had been built purely around the nobility of the ideas they'd discussed.

Armed with these new concepts, John knew now that he would not change jobs. He would stay where he was and work to build a Heroic Environment.

After a long silence, John said, "Kip, I don't know how to thank you for what you've taught me."

Kip smiled and said, "You can thank me by letting me know how you're doing." And then, with special warmth, he added, "John, I think you know that I'm rooting for your success."

"Kip, will you be coming through Denver on one of your future trips?"

"Yes, I'll be passing through in April."

John's eyes lit up. "I'd be honored to have you stay with us."

"That's very kind of you," said Kip, smiling. The two men shook hands and exchanged business cards as the train slowed.

♦ ♦ ♦

After receiving a loving homecoming greeting from his wife, Kathy, and his little girl, Lauren, John and his family hurried away from the platform. Suddenly, he heard his name called. As he turned around, he was surprised to see the president of his company and one of the vice presidents.

"Mr. Williams," he exclaimed with surprise, "what are you doing here?"

"We were in Denver for a meeting at your plant when this blasted snowstorm closed the airport, so the corporate jet is useless. I have to be in Los Angeles in two days, so this is the only alternative."

John smiled. "It's not such a bad alternative, sir. It may take longer, but it's amazing the new perspective a train ride can give. Oh, by the way, where are you sitting?"

The president looked at his ticket. "Compartment 417-C."

Suppressing a smile, John responded simply, "Sir, when you get back to corporate headquarters, I'd like to call you. I believe there'll be a lot for us to talk about."

Do You Work in a Heroic Environment®?

After reading this book, you may want to personally evaluate your work environment. Over the past 10 years, the Lebow Company has been gathering worldwide data on just this subject. On the following pages, a brief survey of your work environment for you to take is included. Following the quiz is an analysis of your answers. Please answer all questions candidly and quickly. Your first response will be your most accurate. If you would like to expand your evaluation to your department or entire office, please give us a call for information on the *full* Values & Attitude Study™ Index.

Quiz Directions:

- Answer each question quickly and honestly.

- Indicate your choice by **circling the number** under each question.

- When you get to the section on MY PERCEPTIONS OF MY WORK ENVIRONMENT, evaluate your organization as you see it *today*.

Please answer the following questions about how important each value is to you in enjoying a productive and meaningful relationship in your work environment and with your co-workers.

PERSONAL NEEDS:

How important are the following qualities to you personally?

Honesty: Having honesty among the organization's employees.

Not important	Somewhat important	Important	Very important
0 1 2	3 4 5	6 7 8	9 10

Truth: Always telling the truth within the organization.

Not important	Somewhat important		Important		Very important	
0	1 2	3 4	5 6	7 8	9	10

Trust: Trusting the employees.

Not important	Somewhat important		Important		Very important	
0	1 2	3 4	5 6	7 8	9	10

New ideas: Being open and receptive to new ideas.

Not important	Somewhat important		Important		Very important	
0	1 2	3 4	5 6	7 8	9	10

Risk-taking: Taking the risk to present your ideas or beliefs even if not everyone agrees.

Not important	Somewhat important		Important		Very important	
0	1 2	3 4	5 6	7 8	9	10

Giving credit: Giving credit where credit is due.

Not important	Somewhat important		Important		Very important	
0	1 2	3 4	5 6	7 8	9	10

Selfless behavior: Putting the interests of others first.

Not important   Somewhat important   Important   Very important

0   1   2   3   4   5   6   7   8   9   10

Mentoring: Taking the time needed to teach and help others.

Not important   Somewhat important   Important   Very important

0   1   2   3   4   5   6   7   8   9   10

Please add up your score of circled numbers: _____

Next, divide your score by 8. Your Personal Needs number is:_____ (A).

Now, please continue to identify your organization's present capacity to deliver Heroic values to you and your associates.

MY PERCEPTIONS OF MY WORK ENVIRONMENT:

Evaluate the organization's general performance in regard to the following qualities:

Honesty: Having honesty among the organization's employees.

Not important   Somewhat important   Important   Very important
0   1   2   3   4   5   6   7   8   9   10

Truth: Always telling the truth within the organization.

Not important   Somewhat important   Important   Very important
0   1   2   3   4   5   6   7   8   9   10

Trust: Trusting the employees.

Not important   Somewhat important   Important   Very important
0   1   2   3   4   5   6   7   8   9   10

New ideas: Being open and receptive to new ideas.

Not important   Somewhat important   Important   Very important
0   1   2   3   4   5   6   7   8   9   10

Risk-taking: Taking the risk to present your ideas or beliefs even if not everyone agrees.

Not important   Somewhat important   Important   Very important
0   1   2   3   4   5   6   7   8   9   10

Giving credit: Giving credit where credit is due.

Not important Somewhat important Important Very important
0   1   2   3   4   5   6   7   8   9   10

Selfless behavior: Putting the interests of others first.

Not important Somewhat important Important Very important
0   1   2   3   4   5   6   7   8   9   10

Mentoring: Taking the time needed to teach and help others.

Not important Somewhat important Important Very important
0   1   2   3   4   5   6   7   8   9   10

Please add up your score of circled numbers: _____

Next, divide your score by 8. Perception of Your Work Environment:_____(B).

DEFINING YOUR VTI SCORE

Now take your Personal Needs score _____ (A) and subtract your Perceptions of Your Work Environment score _____ (B) = _____ (C).

Now multiply (C) by 8 = _____ (D). This is your Value Tension Index (VTI).

Value Tension Index™ explanation

Building a Heroic Environment® requires that everyone share the same values. The following benchmarks were established over the past eight years and seem to be accurate on all four continents. Seventeen million surveys were initially conducted in forty countries around the world. Your score should mesh with our experience.

We have lots of experience in doing this with hundreds of organizational sites, so feel free to give us a call. For more information, please contact us directly at 1 (800) 423-9327 in the United States, or fax us at (206) 828-3552. You can also contact us on the Internet at: http://www.heroic environment.com.

VTI range analysis

ABOVE-AVERAGE VTI SCORES:

6-11 Scores in this range suggest a fun place to work where people are respected for their diversity. You will normally have a harmonious group of co-workers who share your values. High levels of productivity are enjoyed. People are listened to, leadership is shared, and creativity flourishes.

12-16 Your company is a nice place to work. Several of your values are not completely shared, but our experience suggests that frank and open conversations about these eight values will provide some healthy perspective on each value. Making requests and not registering complaints will be a productive approach to reducing the VTI score in the future. Leaps in productivity and team spirit are possible.

MID-RANGE VTI SCORES:

17-21 You are now reaching the average range of the VTI scores we register. This category is the "swing" category. We have witnessed improvements of 30 percent or more once these eight values are discussed with candor. We suggest that you begin the conversation by building consensus around a willingness to "experiment for a certain period of time." This will be a step in the right direction.

22-26   Scores in this range are higher than we like; they make up the lower end of the average rating. Tom Peters suggested that most businesses run their operation at a C-grade level. He was talking about the work environment as well as the productivity level. Take this score seriously. Scores in this range suggest that the Navigators have been silenced and the *tracking motors* are turned off!

DANGEROUSLY HIGH VTI SCORES:

27-31   When an organization runs in this range, anything can happen. The organization is in jeopardy of imploding. If you aren't unionized, you will be. If you already have a collective bargaining group, you are wasting a great deal of time in an adversarial environment. Turnover may be higher than you like. Retaining good people is difficult, and the customer is not being well-served. Astonishing opportunities await you if you can turn the VTI numbers around. If any organization could use Heroic principles, yours could. Don't give up. You have a lot of work to do and it will be worth it!

32-37   If you scored your organization in this range, you are probably already looking for another job. This number range is serious. Dramatic action needs to be taken. You have enough Dissidents, Fallen Heroes, and Mavericks to start a revolution. Take this seriously.

A Special Thanks

The information contained in this tale is a result of research begun in 1972 at the University of Chicago. During this period 17,000,000 surveys from 40 countries were completed. 2.4 million of these people were from the United States. The research included senior managers, middle managers, supervisors, and staff personnel from 32 different industrial sectors. It is from these expressed needs that the Heroic Environment's® Eight Principles or Values sprang.

Services Available

Shared Values Report:

The Values & Attitude Study™

The report norms 500 completed private and governmental sites on the 27 indices of the international work environment. Included in this comprehensive report are company totals and management/nonmanagement needs and perceptions; male/female management/nonmanagement contrasts in the context of Values, Job Satisfiers, Behavior Modes, Preferences, and Organizational Systemics. National

Value Tension Index™ Scores and World Class Value Preference™ Scores highlight the report accompanied with both numeric and graphic descriptions in each category. You may order the report on hard copy as well as disk.

Training Services:

The Lebow Company offers complete training services in the areas of the Shared Values Process™ Operating System, Value-Based Consensus Building™ and Value-Based Responsibility Taking™, Value-Based Decision-Making™, and Process Team Development. In addition to full programs workshops, videotapes and Train-the-Trainer Programs are available.

Speeches:

Please ask about keynote addresses by Rob Lebow.

New Distributor Inquiries:

Distributor opportunities are available for qualified consulting and training organizations worldwide to install the Shared Values Process™ or Heroic Environment® Value-Based Operating System in their existing client base.

The Lebow Company
11820 Northup Way/Suite E-101
Bellevue, WA 98005

1 (800) 423-9327
(206) 828-3509
(206) 828-3552 FAX

Internet address: http://www.heroicenvironment.com

E-mail address: Lebow@nwlink.com